Beowulf
and
The Fight at Finnsburh

PUBLICATIONS

Books:

The Dream of the Rood and Cyn(e)wulf and Other Critical Essays, Llanerch (1998) [includes articles on poetry and prose translation from Catalan, Galician and Spanish, autobiography, hagiography, dialectology and social history]

Sixty-five Anglo-Saxon Riddles, Llanerch (1998)

Salvador Espriu. Selected Poems, Translated from the Catalan, Carcanet (1997)

Three Anglo-Saxon Battle Poems, Llanerch (1995)

Anglo-Saxon Didactic Verse, Llanerch (1995)

Anglo-Saxon Elegiac Verse, Llanerch (1994)

Anglo-Saxon Verse Charms, Maxims & Heroic Legends, Anglo-Saxon Books (1993); reprinted, Llanerch (1999)

Anglo-Saxon Verse Runes, Llanerch (1992)

Chiaroscuro, Spendthrift (1991)

The Battles of Maldon and Brunanburh, Llanerch (1991)

Seven Anglo-Saxon Elegies, Llanerch (1991)

Anglo-Saxon Riddles, Llanerch (1990)

A Long Time Waiting, Outposts (1979)

[Plus assorted poems in literary journals in UK, USA, Canada, Spain, 1981–7; and 25 electronic titles published by NoSpine.com]

Joint authored with Josetua Bernet de Rodrigues:

Short Story Translation: from Theory to Practice [seven stories by Saki translated into Spanish], Universidad de Córdoba (1992)

OECD Macrothesaurus – Spanish Version (updating and translating Preface, Introduction, User's Guide and Appendix, 1991)

Collin's Spanish–English Dictionary, Third Version (updating commercial terminology, 1989–90)

Dictionary of Spanish Idioms, Harrap (1991)

Spanish Idioms: Study Aids, Harrap (1990)

Spanish Synonyms: Study Aids, Harrap (1990)

Glossary of Spanish–English Commercial and Industrial Terms, Harrap (1990)

BEOWULF AND THE FIGHT AT FINNSBURH

A Modern English Verse Rendering

by

LOUIS J RODRIGUES

with illustrations by
R. D. FARLEY

RUNETREE PRESS
LONDON
MMII

Published by

RUNETREE PRESS
PO Box 1035
London
W2 6ZX

Typeset and designed from the disc of the author by
Shaun Tyas

Printed and bound in the United Kingdom by
The Book Factory,
1A Mildmay Avenue
London N1 4RS

ISBN

1 898577 08 0

CONTENTS

PREFACE

In my preface to *Anglo-Saxon Religious Verse Allegories* (Llanerch Publishers, 1996) I stated that that work was intended for a non-academic audience with no great pretensions to a profound knowledge of the complexities of Anglo-Saxon versification, syntax, diction or whatever else the pseudo-academic reviewer felt obliged to cite had not been adequately accounted for in those renderings. I repeat that statement once again in connection with the present work, since it is also aimed at the same sort of audience – not because it is easier to please since it is less likely to know better but because it is more interested in enjoying a good tale told well that is at the same time a faithful representation of the original. I have always striven to distinguish clearly between acts of creation and those of re-creation and to assign the credit for inspiration of the latter to the undeniable stimulus of the former. To put it bluntly, the validity of the renderings must be measured against their accurate (or otherwise) reflection of the source of their inspiration.

For the opportunity, at long last, to publish these parallel-text renderings of *Beowulf* and *The Fight at Finnsburh*, I must thank my editor, Rose Heaword of Runetree Press. I must also thank Shaun Tyas for the typesetting and Bob Farley for the excellent illustrations that accompany the texts.

Finally, for their belief in the success of this, my latest venture, I must thank my wife Josefina and son Marc.

LJR
Cambridge, 2001

To my son Marc

Wyrd oft nereð
unfægne eorl, þonne his ellen deah.

INTRODUCTION

Beowulf is the editorial title of a long heroic poem considered the supreme achievement of Anglo-Saxon poetry because of its length (3182 lines) and sustained high quality, although it may be thought to have been surpassed in individual excellences by parts of some of the shorter quasi-lyrical 'elegies' such as *The Wanderer* and *The Seafarer*.

Briefly, it is the poetic presentation of a man Beowulf as the ideal example of Germanic heroic culture, treated for a Christian audience with an explicit symbolism of the conflict of man with the powers of evil. In its dramatic portrayal of moments of high adventure and tragedy in the life of its hero, it employs parallelism, contrast, and a kind of tragic irony through allusive echoes of Germanic heroic lays and historic traditions well-known to its listeners. It has something of the depth and tone of an epic but not the form and construction commonly associated with that ancient classical term. Through Germanic history, legend, and folklore in a style and diction that sustains the best qualities of 'classical Anglo-Saxon verse', it presents a universally appealing tragedy of the human predicament.

The sole surviving manuscript, in which *Beowulf* was copied along with *Judith*, belongs to the tenth or early eleventh century. Although written in Late West Saxon which was the literary *koine* of the period, the poem is presumed to have originated either in Northumbria or Mercia. Generally called the *Beowulf Manuscript*, and also containing three prose pieces (*The Passion of St Christopher*, *The Wonders of the East*, and *The Letter of Alexander to Aristotle*), it was bound up early in the seventeenth century with another twelfth century manuscript containing chiefly King Alfred's adaptation of St Augustine's *Soliloquies*. Laurence Nowell, Dean of Lichfield, whose signature appears on the fly-leaf may have been responsible for its re-discovery after the dissolution of the monasteries. The combined manuscript was catalogued in the library of Sir Robert Cotton under the press-mark Vitellius A.xv and passed into the possession of the British Museum on his death in 1631. It later suffered scorching during the disastrous fire that destroyed part of the Cottonian collection in 1731. This left the edges of the manuscript brittle, and fragments continued to break off until the folios were mounted in paper frames and rebound in the later nineteenth century. What is now the official foliation of the manuscript was added in 1884; this replaced the 'old' foliation, which did not include three leaves inserted at the beginning of the manuscript, and which was made at a time when two leaves of *Beowulf* were displaced from their correct position.

The section of MS Cotton Vitellius A.xv in which *Beowulf* is preserved was written by two scribes, the first of whom copied as far as *Beowulf* 1939 *scyran*, and the second from 1939 *moste* to the end. The division is reflected in the language of the poem, for the forms used by the second scribe diverge in some respects from those of the first: words spelt with *eo* in the earlier part of the manuscript, for instance, often show *io* in the work of the second scribe.

Before the Cottonian fire, Humfrey Wanley had prepared a transcript of lines 1–19 and 53–73 of *Beowulf*, and this provides some limited evidence of readings that have since been lost. Much more important, however, are two complete transcripts of the manuscript made in the later 1780s, now generally known as Thorkelin A and B; the former undertaken by a copyist on behalf of the Icelander Grímur Jónsson Thorkelin, and B by Thorkelin himself. According to Thorkelin both transcripts were made in 1787, though, as Kiernan has argued, it is possible that B was prepared two or three years later than this. At any rate it is apparent that A was undertaken before B, since, according to Malone, some of the readings that were visible to the copyist of A had evidently disappeared when B was made.

Some stylistic characteristics of the poem suggest that it is likely to have been composed in writing and is of monastic origin because the art of composing an extended narrative such as *Beowulf*, markedly reflective and meditative in character, seems unlikely to have developed except within monastic culture, which provided the conditions for sustained composition influenced by Latin literature.

The chief human protagonists in *Beowulf* are Scandinavian peoples: the Danes, prominent in the earlier part of the poem, who endure the marauding attacks of Grendel until both the monster and its avenging mother are overcome by Beowulf; the Geats, of whom Beowulf afterwards becomes king and in whose defence he meets his death in battle against a fire-breathing dragon; and the Swedes, whose conflicts with the Geats are recounted in passages interwoven into the narrative in the later part of the poem.

The narrative material found in *Beowulf* concerning the Danes, the Geats, and the Swedes has analogues in a number of sources, notably the Anglo-Saxon poem *Widsith*, Snorri Sturluson's *Ynglinga saga*, and the Latin work known as *Gesta Danorum* by the Dane Saxo Grammaticus.

The Fight at Finnsburh

The forty-eight line fragment known as *The Fight at Finnsburh*, owes its existence to a copy made by George Hickes of a single isolated folio which he found in a volume of homilies, probably of the thirteenth century, in the London palace of the Archbishop of Canterbury at Lambeth, and published in his *Linguarum Veterum Septentrionalium Thesaurus* (Oxford, 1705). As Hickes' free transcription has also disappeared, his printed version is its sole authoritative source. The text appears to date from the eleventh century and was evidently part of a lay, of which this fragment occurred near the beginning, while another version of a later portion occurs as a lay recited by King Hrothgar's *scop* in *Beowulf* (1063–1159). This vivid and dramatic poem treats of a tragic feud between Danes and Frisians centred on Finnsburh, the fortified dwelling of Finn, the leader of the Frisians.

The story is as follows. A long-standing feud between Danes and Frisians had apparently been settled by a marriage between Hildeburh, a princess of a tribe closely connected with the Danes, and Finn, who, while himself a Jute, ruled the Frisians from his stronghold Finnsburh, situated just outside Friesland. The

Hocingas, a tribe to which Hildeburh belonged, may have been ethnically Jutes yet subjects of the Danish king Thus the alliance could have been the easier to forge because both Finn and Hildeburh were of Jutish origin, though members of different tribes. The fact that the feud which was to be renewed after this attempted reconciliation would be between Jutish warriors on either side, who were compelled to it by the supreme duty of revenge, would add tragic poignancy to the tale. For the obligation to avenge a slain leader, a matter of *comitatus* loyalty, took priority over the loyalty of blood-relationship. When Hildeburh's sons were grown enough to bear arms, her brother Hnæf, leader of the 'Half-Danes' ('Jutes' or Danes'), had occasion to visit her and her husband King Finn, accompanied by sixty retainers. These guests, while asleep in the hall of Finnsburh after having been well entertained, were suddenly attacked by Finn's men and Hnæf, as well as his sister's sons, along with many warriors on both sides, was slain. But Hengest, who succeeded Hnæf as leader of the Half-Danes, had by then got himself with his men into some strongly protected position from which they could not have been dislodged except with more loss of Finn's Jutes than he could risk. So Finn accepted a truce, proposed by Hengest, that they have a great ceremonial funeral for the dead of both sides, and then Hengest and his men would, at least for the winter, become Finn's followers. As members of his *comitatus*, Finn promised them the same excellent treatment he accorded his own Frisian warriors. Hengest's motive seems to have been revenge, which could be more surely carried out if he gained a respite by this postponement. Hengest is most likely to have suffered a profound mental struggle, torn as he was between the heinousness of accepting service with Finn, whose people had slain his own leader Hnæf, and the basic Germanic duty of exacting vengeance for Hnæf. After spending the winter with Finn, who was probably not responsible for the initial outbreak of the fighting, Hengest, taunted by some of his men, plans vengeance deliberately, thus ignoring the new allegiance to Finn which his joining his *comitatus* implied. The fight is renewed by some of Hengest's followers acting as *agents provocateurs*, and Finn and all his men are slain. Hildeburh, also perhaps glad of this vengeance, though distraught with the conflicting loyalty to her husband Finn, is taken back to her homeland by the victorious Danes.

This tragic tale, so vividly illustrating conflicting Germanic heroic loyalties, is evidently told in its original lay to an audience entirely familiar with its subject-matter. Only the crises, the highlights and dramatic moments, are touched upon, and this very allusively. Hence the unravelling of the details must remain a puzzle to us today. The original lay of *The Fight at Finnsburh* must have been much older than the fragment: and later parts of it treated in a seemingly more advanced style in 'The Tale of Finn' in *Beowulf*. Yet, while the style and tone of the fragment suggest an early date, the occasional irregularities of its metre would point to a later period. Both Finn and Hnæf are mentioned in *Widsith* (27, 29), which suggests that their story was well-known on the Germanic Continent and in England. Most of the fragment is in dramatic direct speech but lines 34–42 is a piece of heroic narrative showing the earliest expression of the Germanic spirit at its best and most moving.

A Note on the Text and Rendering

My construction of the text is based on the version of Klaeber, supplemented by the suggestions of Wrenn, Kiernan and Jack.

Anglo-Saxon (or Old English) is not a very difficult language, though it is neglected by many of those concerned with the long period of its history during which it was spoken and written. But the idiom and diction of its verse is not easy. Its manner and conventions, and its metre, are unlike those of modern English verse of which it is the historical predecessor. Also preserved fragmentarily and by chance, it was only during the late nineteenth and early twentieth centuries that it was redeciphered and interpreted, without the aid of any tradition or gloss: for, in England, unlike Iceland, the old poetic tradition of the North was at length completely broken and buried.

Consequently many words and phrases are met rarely or only once. This is the case, for example, with *eoten* "giant" which is only found in *Beowulf* (112). This word was well known, according to other available evidence, but it is only in *Beowulf* that it is recorded in its Anglo-Saxon form, because this poem alone has survived of the oral and written matter concerning such legends.

Descriptive compounds, such as *sundwudu*, literally "swimming-timber" for "ship" (208) and *swan-rad*, literally "swan's road" for "sea" (200) are instances of figurative usage of the language and a frequent poetical device often resorted to, instead of such ordinary words as "ship" and "sea", which present a second difficulty.

The diction of *Beowulf* was poetical, archaic, artificial at the time that the poem was composed and many words used by the ancient English poets had, even in the eighth century, already passed out of colloquial use for anything from a lifetime to hundreds of years. Some words had never, in the senses given to them by the poets, been used in ordinary language at all. This does not apply solely to poetical devices such as *swan-rad*; it is also true of some simple and much used words, such as *beorn* (211) and *freca* (1563). Both meant "warrior" or in heroic poetry "man". That is to say, both were used for "warrior" by poets, while *beorn* was still a form for the word "bear" and *freca* a name of the "wolf"; they were still used in verse when their original senses were forgotten. To use *beorn* and *freca* instead of "man" made the language "poetical"; but, their use long after much else of the ancient diction had perished also made them "archaic".

Variation, resulting from the long list of synonyms, or partial equivalents to denote things with which Northern heroic verse was specially concerned – such as the sea, and ships, and swords, and especially men (warriors and sailors), is sometimes impossible to match in modern English. For "man" in *Beowulf*, for instance, there appear at least ten virtual synonyms: *beorn*, *ceorl*, *freca*, *guma*, *hæleð* and *hæle*, *leod*, *mann* and *manna*, *rinc*, *secg*, and *wer*. Not all of these, however, are strictly synonymous, since *ceorl*, *mann*, and *wer* were also current words with proper senses: freeman, human being, adult male or husband. This list can be extended to at least twenty-five items by inclusion of words whose sense remained in varying degrees more specific, though in heroic verse they could as a rule replace the simple *mann*: words implying noble birth such as *æðeling* and *eorl*; meaning youths or young men, such as *cniht*, *hyse*, *maga*, *mecg*; or denoting the various companions, followers, and servants of lords and kings, such as *gædeling, geneat, gesið, scealc, ðegn*; or explicitly signifying "warrior", such as *cempa, oretta, wiga, wigend.*

As regards my rendering in general, I have endeavoured to present as close an approximation to the meaning of the original Anglo-Saxon as possible but have opted for a loosely "alliterative" metre corresponding roughly to Sievers' six patterns or types: falling-falling (A); rising-rising (B); clashing (C); falling by stages (Da); or broken fall (Db); and fall and rise (E) according to which he classified most lines of Anglo-Saxon verse.

More difficult is the problem of syntax since the verse is written continuously like prose and the punctuation is sparing, if not non-existent. Be that as it may, my aim has been to reflect the style of the original as far as the language will allow without being awkwardly inappropriate.

Grendel's Mother

BEOWULF

BEOWULF

Hwæt, we Gar-Dena   in geardagum, [f.132r]
þeodcyninga   þrym gefrunon,
hu ða æþelingas   ellen fremedon.
Oft Scyld Scefing   sceaþena þreatum,
monegum mægþum,   meodosetla ofteah,
egsode eorl[as],   syððan ærest wearð
feasceaft funden;   he þæs frofre gebad,
weox under wolcnum,   weorðmyndum þah,
oðþæt him æghwylcþ[ær]   ymbsittendra
ofer hronrade   hyran scolde,
gomban gyldan.   Þæt wæs god cyning!
Ðæm eafera wæs   æfter cenned
geong in geardum,   þone God sende
folce to frofre;   fyrenðearfe ongeat
þ[e] hie ær drugon   aldor[le]ase
lange hwile.   Him þæs Liffrea,
wuldres Wealdend   woroldare forgeaf;
Beowulf wæs breme   —blæd wide sprang—
Scyldes eafera   Scedelandum in.
Swa sceal [geong g]uma   gode gewyrcean,
fromum feohgiftum,   on fæder | [bea]rme, [f.132v]
þæt hine on ylde   eft gewunigen
wilgesiþas   þonne wig cume,
leode gelæsten;   lofdædum sceal
in mægþa gehwære   man geþeon.
Him ða Scyld gewat   to gescæphwile,
felahror feran   on Frean wære.
Hi hyne þa ætbæron   to brimes faroðe,
swæse gesiþas,   swa he selfa bæd,
þenden wordum weold   wine Scyldinga;
leof landfruma   lange ahte.
Þær æt hyðe stod   hringedstefna
isig ond utfus,   æþelinges fær;
aledon þa   leofne þeoden,

BEOWULF

Well, we have heard tell of the glory of the kings [f.132r]
of the Spear-Danes, how in former times
those princes performed courageous deeds.
Oft Scyld Scefing seized mead-benches
from troops of foes, from many tribes,
terrified their eorls, after he was first
found destitute; he was comforted for that,
thrived under the heavens, prospered in honour,
until each one of the neighbouring nations,
over the whale-road, had to obey him,
yield tribute. He was an able king!
Later, an infant son was born to him,
in his dwelling, whom God had sent
to comfort the folk; he saw the sore need
which they formerly suffered, lacking a lord,
for a long while. To him, therefore, the Lord of life,
the Ruler of glory, gave worldly renown;
Beowulf was renowned, widespread the fame
of the son of Scyld in the Northlands.
So ought a young man by good deeds,
generous gifts in his father's | house, [f.132v]
to ensure that afterwards, in later life,
dear friends stand by him, people serve
him when war comes; by worthy deeds
a man shall thrive in every tribe.
Then, at his fated hour, Scyld, full of strength,
passed on into the Lord's protection.
Beloved comrades bore him down to the sea,
as he himself had bidden them do, when he,
the Scyldings' friend, still ruled with words;
dear lord of the land for long he reigned.
There, in the harbour, the prince's ring-prowed
ship stood, ice-covered and ready to set out;
then they laid down their beloved lord,

beaga bryttan   on bearm scipes,
mærne be mæste. Þær wæs madma fela
of feorwegum,   frætwa gelæded;
ne hyrde ic cymlicor   ceol gegyrwan
hildewæpnum   ond heaðowædum,
billum ond byrnum;   him on bearme læg
madma mænigo,   þa him mid scoldon
on flodes æht   feor gewitan.
Nalæs hi hine læssan   lacum teodan,
þeodgestreonum,   þon þa dydon
þe hine æt frumsceafte   forð onsendon
ænne ofer yðe   umborwe | sende. [f.133r]
Þa gyt hie him asetton   segen g[yl]denne
heah ofer heafod,   leton holm beran,
geafon on garsecg.   Him wæs geomor sefa,
murnende mod.   Men ne cunnon
secgan to soðe,   seleræden[d]e,
hæleð under heofenum,   hwa þæm hlæste onfeng.
I Ða wæs on burgum   Beowulf Scyldinga,
leof leodcyning   longe þrage
folcum gefræge   —fæder ellor hwearf,
aldor of earde—   oþþæt him eft onwoc
heah Healfdene;   heold þenden lifde
gamol ond guðreouw   glæde Scyldingas.
Ðæm feower bearn   forðgerimed
in worold wocun,   weoroda ræswa[n],
Heorogar ond Hroðgar   ond Halga til;
hyrde ic þæt [.....   wæs On]elan cwen,
Heaðo-Scilfingas   healsgebedda.
Þa wæs Hroðgare   heresped gyfen,
wiges weorðmynd,   þæt him his winemagas
georne hyrdon,   oððþæt seo geogoð geweox,
magodriht micel.   Him on mod bearn
þæt healreced   hatan wolde,
medoærn micel   men gewyrcean, [f.133v]
þone yldo bearn   æfre gefrunon,
ond þær on innan   eall gedælan
geongum ond ealdum,   swylc him God sealde,
buton folcscare   ond feorum gumena.
Ða ic wide gefrægn   weorc gebannan
manigre mægþe   geond þisne middangeard,
folcstede frætwan.   Him on fyrste gelomp,
ædre mid yldum,   þæt hit wearð ealgearo,
healærna mæst;   scop him Heort naman
se þe his wordes geweald   wide hæfde.
He beot ne aleh,   beagas dælde,

bestower of rings, in the bosom of the barge,
renowned by the mast. Much treasure there was,
precious gear fetched from distant parts;
I have not heard of a comelier keel adorned
with weapons of war and battle gear,
blades and byrnies; on his breast lay
a multitude of treasures, that were to go far
with him into the power of the flood.
They provided him with no lesser gifts,
and royal treasures, than did those
who, in the beginning, sent him forth
alone over the waves, child as he | was. [f.133r]
Furthermore, they set up a golden standard
high above his head, allowed the sea to bear him,
gave him to the ocean; sad were their spirits,
mournful their minds. Hall-counsellors,
warriors under the heavens cannot tell
truly who received that cargo.
I Then in the strongholds was Beowulf of the Scyldings,
beloved king of the people for a long time
famous among folk —his father had gone hence,
the lord from his land— until later to him was born
tall Healfdene; while he lived he ruled,
old and fierce in battle, the gracious Scyldings.
To him, four children in succession
were born in the world, to the leader of armies:
Heorogar and Hrothgar, and Halga the Good.
I heard that [... was On]ela's queen,
cherished consort of the Heatho-Scylfing.
Then was Hrothgar given success in war,
glory in battle, so that his friends and kinsmen
willingly obeyed him, until the young warriors grew,
a mighty band of retainers. It came into his mind
that he would command men to construct
a hall, a great(er) mead | -hall [f.133v]
than the children of men had ever heard of
and therein share out
among young and old, whatever God gave him,
except common land and the lives of men.
I have heard orders for the work were then given
far and wide to many nations throughout this world,
to adorn the people's place. In time it happened
swiftly among men, that it was fully ready,
the greatest of halls; he, who ruled by his word
far and wide, gave it the name Heorot.
He left not his vow unfulfilled but shared out rings,

sinc æt symle. Sele hlifade,
heah ond horngeap; heaðowylma bad,
laðan liges; ne wæs hit lenge þa gen
þæt se [e]cghete aþumsw[eo]ran
æfter wælniðe wæcnan scolde.
Ða se ellengæst earfoðlice
þrage geþolode, se þe in þystrum bad,
þæt he dogora gehwam dream gehyrde
hludne in healle; þær wæs hearpan sweg,
swutol sang scopes. Sægde se þe cuþe
frumsceaft fira feorran reccan,
cwæð þæt se Ælmihtiga eorðan worh[te], [f.134r]
wlitebeorhtne wang, swa wæter bebugeð,
gesette sigehreþig sunnan ond monan
leoman to leohte landbuendum,
ond gefrætwade foldan sceatas
leomum ond leafum; lif eac gesceop
cynna gehwylcum þara ðe cwice hwyrfaþ.
Swa ða drihtguman dreamum lifdon
eadiglice, oððæt an ongan
fyrene fre[m]man feond on helle.
Wæs se grimma gæst Grendel haten,
mære mearcstapa, se þe moras heold,
fen ond fæsten; fifelcynnes eard
wonsæli wer wearddode hwile,
siþan him Scyppend forscrifen hæfde
in Caines cynne —þone cwealm gewræc
ece Drihten, þæs þe he Abel slog.

treasure at the feast. The hall towered,
tall and wide-gabled; it awaited the hostile surges
of hateful fire; the time was not yet at hand
when violent hatred between son-in-law
and father-in-law was to arise after deadly enmity.

Then the fierce spirit painfully suffered
torment for a time, he who dwelt in darkness,
in that each day he heard loud revelry
in the hall; there was the sound of the harp,
the clear song of the scop. He spoke, who knew how
to recount the creation of men from long ago, | [f.134r]
told how the Almighty made the earth,
a beautiful plain, which water encircles,
set up in triumph the radiance of sun
and moon, as light for land-dwellers,
and adorned the corners of the earth
with branches and leaves; how also he created life
for every kind of thing that moves and breathes.
Thus these retainers lived in joy,
happily, until a certain fiend from hell
began to perform wicked deeds.
That grim creature was called Grendel,
famed march-rover, who held the moors,
fen and fastness; the unblessed creature
lived for a time in the monsters' lair,
after the Creator had condemned them
as Cain's kin —the eternal Lord avenged
the killing, because he slew Abel.

Ne gefeah he þære fæhðe,   ac he hine feor forwræc,
Metod for þy mane   manycynne fram.
Þanon untydras   ealle onwocon,
eotenas ond ylfe   ond orcneas,
swylce gi|gantas,   þa wið Gode wunnon [f.134v]
lange þrage;   he him ðæs lean forgeald.

II Gewat ða neosian,   syþðan niht becom,
hean huses,   hu hit Hring-Dene
æfter beorþege   gebun hæfdon.
Fand þa ðær inne   æþelinga gedriht
swefan æfter symble;   sorge ne cuðon,
wonsceaft wera.   Wiht unhælo,
grim ond grædig,   gearo sona wæs,
reoc ond reþe,   ond on ræste genam
þritig þegna;   þanon eft gewat
huðe hremig   to ham faran,
mid þære wælfylle   wica neosan.
Ða wæs on uhtan   mid ærdæge
Grendles guðcræft   gumum undyrne;
þa wæs æfter wiste   wop up ahafen,
micel morgensweg.   Mære þeoden,
æþeling ærgod,   unbliðe sæt,
þolode ðryðswyð,   þegnsorge dreah,
syðþan hie þæs laðan   last sceawedon,
wergan gastes;   wæs þæt gewin to strang,
lað ond longsum!   Næs hit lengra fyrst, [f.135r]
ac ymb ane niht   eft gefremede
morðbeala mare,   ond no mearn fore,
fæhðe ond fyrene;   wæs to fæst on þam.
Þa wæs eaðfynde   þe him elles hwær
gerumlicor   ræste [sohte],
bed æfter burum,   ða him gebeacnod wæs,
gesægd soðlice   sweotolan tacne
healðegnes hete;   heold hyne syðþan
fyr ond fæstor   se þæm feonde ætwand.
Swa rixode   ond wið rihte wan,
ana wið eallum,   oðþæt idel stod
husa selest.   Wæs seo hwil micel;
twelf wintra tid   torn geþolode
wine Scyld[i]n[g]a,   weana gehwelcne,
sidra sorga.   Forðam [secgum] wearð,
ylda bearnum   undyrne cuð
gyddum geomore,   þætte Grendel wan
hwile wið Hroþgar,   heteniðas wæg,
fyrene ond fæhðe   fela missera,
singale sæce,   sibbe ne wolde

He got no joy from that feud, but the Creator
drove him far from mankind for that crime.
Thence were born all evil broods,
ogres and elves and evil spirits,
also | giants, who contended with God [f.134v]
a long time; he paid them their reward for that.
II Then, after night had come, he went to seek out
the lofty house, to see how the Ring-Danes
had settled in after their beer-drinking.
Inside he found a band of æthelings
sleeping after the feast; they knew not grief,
the misery of men. The evil creature
was soon ready, grim and greedy,
savage and fierce, and seized thirty thanes
in their resting-place; thence he turned,
exulting in plunder, to go back home,
to seek out his dwelling with that fill of slaughter.
Then, in the half-light just before dawn,
was Grendel's war-strength manifest to men;
then, after the feasting, was lamentation raised,
a great cry in the morning. The famous prince,
an ætheling of proven excellence, sat joyless,
strong in might he suffered, sorrowed for his thanes,
when they examined the track of that loathsome,
accursed spirit; that struggle was too fierce,
grievous and prolonged! After no longer | lapse [f.135r]
than one night, again he wrought
greater slaughter, vengeful acts and wickedness,
and felt no remorse for it; he was too fixed on them.
Then was it easy to find him who elsewhere
sought a resting-place farther away,
a bed among outbuildings, once he was shown
the hall-thane's hatred made manifest
by clear proof; he who escaped the enemy held
himself farther away and more securely afterwards.
Thus he ruled and strove against right,
one against all, until the best of houses
stood empty. This went on for a long while;
twelve winters' space the friend of the Scyldings
endured affliction, every kind of woe,
great grief. Wherefore it became
well-known to the children of men,
sadly in songs, that Grendel had long
waged war on Hrothgar, many half-years
bore fierce hatred, feud, and enmity,
a constant conflict, would not have peace

wið manna hwone   mægenes Deniga,
feorhbealo feorran,   fea þingian;
ne þær nænig witena   wenan þorfte
beorhtre bote   to ban[an] folmum, [f.135v]
[ac se] æglaca   ehtende wæs,
deorc deaþscua   duguþe ond geogoþe
seomade ond syrede,   sinnihte heold
mistige moras;   men ne cunnon
hwyder helrunan   hwyrftum scriþað.
Swa fela fyrena   feond mancynnes
atol angengea   oft gefremede,
heardra hynða;   Heorot eardode,
sincfage sel   sweartum nihtum;
no he þone gifstol   gretan moste,
maþðum for Metode,   ne his myne wisse.
   Þæt wæs wræc micel   wine Scyldinga,
modes brecða.   Monig oft gesæt
rice to rune;   ræd eahtedon,
hwæt swiðferhðum   selest wære
wið færgryrum   to gefremmanne.
Hwilum hie geheton   æt h[æ]rgtrafum
wigweorþunga,   wordum bædon,
þæt him gastbona   geoce gefremede
wið þeodþreaum.   Swylc wæs þeaw hyra,
hæþenra hyht;   helle gemundon
in modsefan,   Metod hie ne cuþon,
dæda Demend,   ne wiston hie Drihten God, [f.136r]
ne hie huru heofena Helm   herian ne cuþon,

with any man of the Danish force,
nor cease from murder, nor settle for money;
nor did any of the counsellors there expect
splendid compensation at the slayer's hands, | [f.135v]
[but the] demon, the dark death-shadow,
was relentless, lay in wait for and ambushed
warriors young and old, in the endless night held
the misty moors; men do not know
whither demons go in their wanderings.
Thus mankind's foe, the fearful solitary,
often perpetrated many malicious deeds,
sore injuries; on dark nights he inhabited
Heorot, the richly decorated hall;
he was not permitted to approach the throne,
that treasure, because of the Ruler, and felt not his love.
  That was great misery for the friend of the Scyldings,
heart-breaking grief. Often many a man
of high rank sat in council; considered
what were best for strong-minded men
to do against the terror of sudden attacks.
Sometimes at heathen temples they vowed
homage to idols, petitioned with prayers
that the slayer of souls should succour them
for the nation's calamities. Such was their custom,
the hope of the heathen; they remembered hellish things
in their minds. They knew not the Creator,
Judge of deeds, they knew not the Lord God, | [f.136r]
nor, indeed, how to praise the Protector of heaven,

wuldres Waldend. Wa bið þæm ðe sceal
þurh sliðne nið   sawle bescufan
in fyres fæþm,   frofre ne wenan,
wihte gewendan. Wel bið þæm þe mot
æfter deaðdæge   Drihten secean
ond to Fæder fæþmum   freoðo wilnian.

III Swa ða mælceare   maga Healfdenes
singala seað. Ne mihte snotor hæleð
wean onwendan;   wæs þæt gewin to swyð,
laþ ond longsum,   þe on ða leode becom,
nydwracu niþgrim,   nihtbealwa mæst,
   Þæt fram ham gefrægn   Higelaces þegn
god mid Geatum,   Grendles dæda;
se wæs moncynnes   mægenes strengest
on þæm dæge   þysses lifes,
æþele ond eacen. Het him yðlidan
godne gegyrwan;   cwæð, he guðcyning
ofer swanrade   secean wolde,
mærne þeoden,   þa him wæs manna þearf.
Ðone siðfæt him   snotere ceorlas
lythwon logon,   þeah he him leof wære; [f.136v]
hwetton hige[r]ofne,   hæl sceawedon.
Hæfde se goda   Geata leoda
cempan gecorone   þara þe he cenoste
findan mihte;   fiftyna sum
sundwudu sohte,   secg wisade,
lagucræftig mon   landgemyrcu.
Fyrst forð gewat;   flota wæs on yðum,
bat under beorge. Beornas gearwe
on stefn stigon;   streamas wundon,
sund wið sande. Secgas bæron
on bearm nacan   beorhte frætwe,
guðsearo geatolic;   guman ut scufon,
weras on wilsið   wudu bundenne.
Gewat þa ofer wægholm   winde gefysed
flota famiheals   fugle gelicost,
oðþæt ymb antid   oþres dogores
wundenstefna   gewaden hæfde
þæt ða liðende   land gesawon,
brimclifu blican,   beorgas steape,
side sænæssas;   þa wæs sund liden,
eole[t] æt ende. Þanon up hraðe
Wedera leode   on wang stigon,
sæwudu sældon;   syrcan hrysedon,
guðgewædo. Gode þancedon
þæs þe him yþlade   eaðe wurdon.

the Ruler of glory. Woe is it to him who must
in terrible hostility thrust his soul
into the fire's embrace, not hope for comfort,
change in any way. Well is it for him who is allowed
after his death-day to seek the Lord
and ask for protection in the Father's embrace.

III So, on the sorrow of the time, the son of Healfdene
brooded constantly. Nor could the wise warrior
set aside his woes, the struggle was too harsh,
hateful and prolonged, which had befallen the people,
cruel, dire distress, greatest of night-evils.

In his homeland, a thane of Hygelac's,
excellent among the Geats, heard of Grendel's deeds;
he was the greatest in strength among men
at that time in this life,
noble and mighty. He ordered a good ship
to be prepared for him; said he would seek
the war-king, the famous prince,
over the swan's road, since he had need of men.
Wise men found very little fault with him
for that venture, | though he was dear to them; [f.136v]
they encouraged the valiant man, examined the omens.
From the people of the Geats the hero
had chosen warriors, the bravest
he could find; with fourteen others
he sought the ship, a man skilled
in sea-craft led the way to the shore.
Time passed on; the ship was on the waves,
the boat under the cliff. The warriors, equipped,
climbed on the prow; currents eddied,
sea against sand. Men bore
into the bosom of the ship bright trappings,
splendid war-gear; the men shoved out
the well-braced ship, warriors on a willing journey.
Then, over the sea, driven on by the wind,
flew the foamy-necked ship, most like a bird,
until in due course on the following day
its curved prow had come to where
the voyagers could sight land,
shining sea-cliffs, steep crags,
broad headlands; then was the sea crossed,
the voyage at an end. Quickly thence
the men of the Weders stepped ashore,
moored the sea-vessel; mail-shirts shook,
war garments. They thanked God
that the sea-path had been easy for them. | [f.137r]

Þa of wealle geseah   weard Scildinga, [f.137r]
se þe holmclifu   healdan scolde,
beran ofer bolcan   beorhte randas,
fyrdsearu fuslicu;   hine fyrwyt bræc
modgehygdum   hwæt þa men wæron.
Gewat him þa to waroðe   wicge ridan
þegn Hroðgares,   þrymmum cwehte
mægenwudu mundum,   meþelwordum frægn:
'Hwæt syndon ge   searohæbbendra,
byrnum werede,   þe þus brontne ceol
ofer lagustræte   lædan cwomon,
hider ofer holmas?   [Ic hwi]le wæs
endesæta,   ægwearde heold,
þe on land Dena   laðra nænig
mid scipherge   sceðþan ne meahte.
No her cuðlicor   cuman ongunnon
lindhæbbende,   ne ge leafnesword
guðfremmendra   gearwe ne wisson,
maga gemedu.   Næfre ic maran geseah
eorla ofer eorþan   ðonne ic eower sum,
secg on searwum.   Nis þæt seldguma
wæpnum geweorðad   —næfre him his wlite leoge,
ænlic ansyn!   Nu ic eower sceal
frumcyn witan,   ær ge fyr heonan [f.137v]
leassceaweras   on land Dena
furþur feran.   Nu ge feorhbuend,
mereliðende,   min[n]e gehyrað
anfealdne geþoht: ofost is selest
to gecyðanne,   hwanan eowre cyme syndon.'
IIII Him se yldesta   andswarode,
werodes wisa,   wordhord onleac:
'We synt gumcynnes   Geata leode
ond Higelaces   heorðgeneatas.
Wæs min fæder   folcum gecyþed,
æþele ordfruma,   Ecgþeow haten;
gebad wintra worn   ær he on weg hwurfe,
gamol of geardum;   hine gearwe geman
witena welhwylc   wide geond eorþan.
We þurh holdne hige   hlaford þinne,
sunu Healfdenes   secean cwomon,
leodgebyrgean;   wes þu us larena god!
Habbað we to þæm mæran   micel ærende,
Deniga frean;   ne sceal þær dyrne sum
wesan, þæs ic wene.   Þu wast —gif hit is
swa we soþlice   secgan hyrdon— [f.138r]
þæt mid Scyldingum   sceaðona ic nat hwylc,

Then from the wall the Scyldings' watchman,
whose duty it was to guard the sea-cliffs,
saw bright shields borne over the gangway,
arms ready for use; curiosity of thought
pressed him to know who the men were.
Then Hrothgar's thane, riding on horseback,
went down to the shore, forcefully shook
the mighty shaft in his hands, asked formally:
'What manner of armed men are you,
protected in byrnies, who have come thus,
bringing a tall ship over the sea-road,
hither over the water? For a long time I
have been coastguard, kept sea-watch
so that no foe with a naval force
could inflict harm on the land of the Danes.
Never have shield-bearers more openly
begun to come here, nor knew ye fully
of the war-makers' password
approved by kinsmen. Never have I seen
a mightier eorl on earth than is one of you,
a hero in armour. That is no hall-retainer
exalted with weapons —unless his looks belie him,
his matchless appearance! Now I must
know your origin, rather than ye | hence [f.137v]
as spies in the land of the Danes
go farther. Now ye far-dwellers,
seafarers, listen to my
plain thought: it is best swiftly
to tell from where you are coming.'

IIII To him the chief replied,
the leader of the company, unlocked his word-hoard:
'We are of the people of the Geats
and hearth-companions of Hygelac.
My father was well-known among the nations,
a noble leader at the battle-front called Ecgtheow;
he lived to see many winters, ere he went away,
an old man, from his dwelling; every wise man
readily remembers him widely throughout the earth.
With well-disposed heart we have come
to seek thy lord, the son of Healfdene,
protector of his people; give us good counsel!
We have an important mission to the famous
lord of the Danes; nor shall there be anything
concealed, as I think. Thou knowest —if it is so,
as truly we have heard it said— | [f.138r]
that among the Scyldings I know not what ravagers,

deogol dædhata deorcum nihtum
eaweð þurh egsan uncuðne nið,
hynðu ond hrafyl. Ic þæs Hroðgar mæg
þurh rumne sefan ræd gelæran,
hu he frod ond god feond oferswyðeþ
—gyf him edwend[e]n æfre scolde,
bealuwa bisigu bot eft cuman—
ond þa cearwylmas colran wurðaþ;
oððe a syþðan earfoðþrage,
þreanyd þolað, þenden þær wunað
on heahstede husa selest.'
  Weard maþelode, ðær on wicge sæt,
ombeht unforht: 'Æghwæþres sceal
scearp scyldwiga gescad witan
worda ond worca, se þe wel þenceð.
Ic þæt gehyre, þæt þis is hold weorod
frean Scyldinga. Gewitaþ forð beran
wæpen ond gewædu, ic eow wisige.
Swylce ic maguþegnas mine hate
wið feonda gehwone flotan eowerne,
niwtyrwydne nacan on sande
arum healdan, oþðæt eft byreð
ofer lagustreamas leofne mannan [f.138v]
wudu wundenhals to Wedermearce;
godfremmendra swylcum gifeþe bið
þæt þone hilderæs hal gedigeð.'
  Gewiton him þa feran; flota stille bad,
seomode on s[a]le sidfæþmed scip,
on ancre fæst. Eoforlic scionon
ofer hleorber[g]an gehroden golde,
fah ond fyrheard —ferhwearde heold
guþmod gr[i]mmon. Guman onetton,
sigon ætsomne, oþþæt hy [s]æl timbred,
geatolic ond goldfah ongyton mihton;
þæt wæs foremærost foldbuendum
receda under roderum, on þæm se rica bad;
lixte se leoma ofer landa fela.
Him þa hildedeor [h]of modigra
torht getæhte, þæt hie him to mihton
gegnum gangan; guðbeorna sum
wicg gewende, word æfter cwæð:
'Mæl is me to feran; Fæder alwalda
mid arstafum eowic gehealde
siða gesunde! Ic to sæ wille,
wið wrað werod wearde healdan.' [f.139r]

V Stræt wæs stanfah, stig wisode

what mysterious persecutors on dark nights,
through terror work unheard of malice,
humiliation and carnage. I can give Hrothgar
good counsel about this with a generous heart,
how he, old and wise, may overcome the enemy
—if change is ever to come to him,
relief from the affliction of miseries—
and his surging anxieties grow cooler;
or a time of tribulation ever after
suffer, dire distress, as long as the best
of houses remains there in its lofty place.'
The watchman, fearless officer, spoke
from where he sat on his horse: 'A keen-witted
shield-warrior who thinks clearly must know
the meaning both of words and of deeds.
I understand that this is a company, loyal
to the lord of the Scyldings. Go forth, bear
weapons and armour; I will guide you.
Also, I will order my young thanes to guard
your ship honourably against every enemy,
your newly-tarred vessel on the sand,
until the ship with curved prow
carries its beloved men back again
over | sea-currents to the coast of the Weders; [f.138v]
to such a one who acts nobly may it be granted
that he survives the battle-storm unharmed.'
Then they set off; the ship lay still,
the wide-bottomed ship rested on the rope,
fast at anchor. Figures of boars, adorned
with gold, shone above the cheek-guards,
gleaming and fire-hardened —kept guard over lives
of grim warriors. The men hastened,
advanced together, until they could see
the timbered hall, splendid and decked with gold;
for earth-dwellers that was the most famous
of halls beneath the skies, in which the mighty one dwelt;
its light shone over many lands.
The battle-brave guide pointed out to them
the splendid bright dwelling of proud men,
that they might go directly there; one of the warriors
turned his horse, then spoke words:
'It is time for me to go; may the almighty Father
by his favour keep you safe
in your ventures! I will return to the sea,
to keep watch against | a hostile host.' [f.139r]
V The way was paved, the path led

gumum ætgædere. Guðbyrne scan
heard hondlocen, hringiren scir
song in searwum, þa hie to sele furðum
in hyra gryregeatwum gangan cwomon.
Setton sæmeþe side scyldas,
rondas regnhearde wið þæs recedes weal;
bugon þa to bence —byrnan hringdon,
guðsearo gumena. Garas stodon,
sæmanna searo samod ætgædere,
æscholt ufan græg; wæs se irenþreat
wæpnum gewurþad.
Þa ðær wlonc hæleð
oretmecgas æfter [æþ]e[l]um frægn:
'Hwanon ferigeað ge fætte scyldas,
græge syrcan ond grimhelmas,
heresceafta heap? Ic eom Hroðgares
ar ond ombiht. Ne seah ic elþeodige
þus manige men modiglicran.
Wen' ic þæt ge for wlenco, nalles for wræcsiðum
ac for higeþrymmum Hroðgar sohton.' [f.139v]
Him þa ellenrof andswarode,
wlanc Wedera leod, word æfter spræc
heard under helme: 'We synt Higelaces
beodgeneatas; Beowulf is min nama.
Wille ic asecgan sunu Healfdenes,
mærum þeodne min ærende,
aldre þinum, gif he us geunnan wile,
þæt we hine swa godne gretan moton.'
Wulfgar maþelode —þæt wæs Wendla leod;
wæs his modsefa manegum gecyðed,
wig ond wisdom—: 'Ic þæs wine Deniga,
frean Scildinga frinan wille,
beaga bryttan, swa þu bena eart,
þeoden mærne ymb þinne sið,
ond þe þa andsware ædre gecyðan
ðe me se goda agifan þenceð.'
Hwearf þa hrædlice þær Hroðgar sæt,
eald ond unhar mid his eorla gedriht;
eode ellenrof þæt he for eaxlum gestod
Deniga frean; cuþe he duguðe þeaw.
Wulfgar maðelode to his winedrihtne: [f.140r]
'Her syndon geferede, feorran cumene
ofer geofenes begang Geata leode;
þone yldestan oretmecgas
Beowulf nemnað. Hy benan synt,
þæt hie, þeoden min, wið þe moton

the men together. War-mail shone,
hard hand-linked, bright iron rings
clinked in their armour, when they first came
striding up to the hall in their grim gear.
Sea-weary, they laid broad shields,
wondrous shield-bosses, against the building wall;
then they sank on the bench —byrnies rang out,
war-shirts of men. Spears stood,
stacked together, seamen's arms,
grey-topped ash-wood; the armed troop
was worthy of its weapons.
                                        Then a proud hero there
questioned the warriors about their lineage:
  'Whence bring ye these gold-plated shields,
grey mail-shirts and visored helms,
this heap of battle-shafts? I am Hrothgar's
herald and officer. I have never seen
so many foreigners braver in appearance.
I imagine it is from daring, not from exile,
but | greatness of heart, that ye sought Hrothgar.' [f.139v]
Then the proud prince of the Weders renowned for courage,
answered him, stern beneath his helm,
spoke these words in reply: 'We are Hygelac's
table-companions; Beowulf is my name.
I will declare my mission to the son
of Healfdene, the famous prince,
thy lord, if he will grant us
that we might address his gracious self.'
Wulfgar spoke —he was a man of the Wendels;
his spirit known to many,
his prowess in war and his wisdom—: 'I will ask
the friend of the Danes, the lord of the Scyldings,
bestower of rings, renowned prince,
concerning thy venture, as thou desirest,
and speedily make known to thee the answer
which the gracious one thinks fit to give me.'
  Then he turned swiftly to where Hrothgar sat,
old and quite grey, with his retinue of eorls;
the brave one went forward till he stood squarely before
the lord of the Danes; he knew the custom of the company.
Wulfgar spoke | to his friend and lord: [f.140r]
'Men of the Geats, come from afar,
have travelled here over the sea's expanse;
the warriors call the chief
Beowulf. They request
that they, my prince, may be permitted

wordum wrixlan;   no ðu him wearne geteoh
ðinra gegncwida,   glædman Hroðgar.
Hy on wiggetawum   wyrðe þinceað
eorla geæhtlan;   huru se aldor deah,
se þæm heaðorincum   hider wisade.'
VI   Hroðgar maþelode,   helm Scyldinga:
'Ic hine cuðe   cnihtwesende;
wæs his ealdfæder   Ecgþeo haten,
ðæm to ham forgeaf   Hreþel Geata
angan dohtor;   is his eafor[a] nu
heard her cumen,   sohte holdne wine.
Ðonne sægdon þæt   sæliþende,
þa ðe gifsceattas   Geata fyredon
þyder to þance,   þæt he þritiges   [f.140v]
manna mægencræft   on his mundgripe
heaþorof hæbbe.   Hine halig God
for arstafum   us onsende,
to West-Denum,   þæs ic wen hæbbe,
wið Grendles gryre.   Ic þæm godan sceal
for his modþræce   madmas beodan.
Beo ðu on ofeste,   hat in gan
seon sibbegedriht   samod ætgædere;
gesaga him eac wordum   þæt hie sint wilcuman
Deniga leodum.'   [Þa to dura eode
widcuð hæleð,]   word inne abead:
'Eow het secgan   sigedrihten min,
aldor East-Dena,   þæt he eower æþelu can,
ond ge him syndon   ofer sæwylmas
heardhicgende   hider wilcuman.
Nu ge moton gangan   in eowrum guðg[e]tawum,
under heregriman   Hroðgar geseon;
lætað hildebord   her onbidan,
wudu wælsceaftas   worda geþinges.'
   Aras þa se rica,   ymb hine rinc manig,
þryðlic þegna heap;   sume þær bidon,
heaðoreaf heoldon,   swa him se hearda bebead.   [f.141r]
Snyredon ætsomne   þa secg wisode
under Heorotes hrof;   [heaþorinc eode,]
heard under helme,   þæt he on heo[r]ðe gestod.
Beowulf maðelode   —on him byrne scan,
searonet seowed   smiþes orþancum—:
'Wæs þu, Hroðgar, hal!   Ic eom Higelaces
mæg ond magoðegn;   hæbbe ic mærða fela
ongunnen on geogoþe.   Me wearð Grendles þing
on minre eþeltyrf   undyrne cuð;
secgað sæliðend,   þæt þæs sele stande,

to exchange words with thee; refuse them not
thy answer, gracious Hrothgar.
In their war-gear they appear worthy
of the esteem of eorls; valiant indeed is the chief
who has led these warriors hither.'
VI Hrothgar spoke, helm of the Scyldings:
'I knew him when he was a boy;
his late father was called Ecgtheow;
to him Hrethel of the Geats gave in marriage
his only daughter; now has his son come
here boldly, sought a faithful friend.
Moroever, said seafarers,
who carried gifts for the Geats
thither to please them, that he has the strength
of | thirty men in his hand-grip, [f.140v]
a man brave in battle. Holy God
of his mercy has sent him to us
West Danes, as I hope,
against Grendel's terror. To the great man
I shall offer treasures for his daring.
Do thou make haste, bid them come in
together to see my band of kinsmen;
tell them also with words that they are welcome
to the people of the Danes.' [Then the widely-known warrior
went to the door,] and from within announced these words:
'My victorious lord, chief of the East-Danes,
has bidden me tell you that he knows of your lineage,
and that ye are welcome to him here,
brave-hearted men from over the sea.
Now ye may go in your war-gear,
beneath battle-visors, to see Hrothgar;
leave your war-shields and spears, deadly shafts,
to await here the outcome of your talk.'
The mighty one arose then, many a warrior about him,
a splendid band of thanes; some waited there,
guarded the battle-booty, as the | brave man instructed them. [f.141r]
Together they hastened, as the warrior directed,
under Heorot's roof; [the war-chief advanced,]
bold beneath his helmet, till he stood on the hearth.
Beowulf spoke —on him byrny shone,
mail-coat cunningly linked by a smith's skill—:
'Hail to thee, Hrothgar! I am Hygelac's
kinsman and thane; many daring deeds have I
undertaken in my youth. The affair of Grendel
was made known to me on my native soil;
seafarers say that this hall, the best of buildings,

reced selesta,   rinca gehwylcum
idel ond unnyt   siððan æfenleoht
under heofenes ha[ð]or   beholen weorþeð.
Þa me þæt gelærdon   leode mine,
þa selestan,   snotere ceorlas,
þeoden Hroðgar,   þæt ic þe sohte,
forþan hie mægenes cræft   min[n]e cuþon;
selfe ofersawon   ða ic of searwum cwom,
fah from feondum,   þær ic fife geband,
yðde eotena cyn,   ond on yðum slog
niceras nihtes,   nearoþearfe dreah,
wræc Wedera nið   —wean ahsodon—   [f.141v]
forgrand gramum;   ond nu wið Grendel sceal,
wið þam aglæcan   ana gehegan
ðing wið þyrse!   Ic þe nu ða,
brego Beorht-Dena,   biddan wille,
eodor Scyldinga,   anre bene,
þæt ðu me ne forwyrne,   wigendra hleo,
freowine folca,   nu ic þus feorran com,
þæt ic mote ana   [ond] minra eorla gedryht,
þes hearda heap,   Heorot fælsian.
Hæbbe ic eac geahsod,   þæt se æglæca
for his wonhydum   wæpna ne recceð.
Ic þæt þonne forhicge   —swa me Higelac sie,
min mondrihten   modes bliðe—
þæt ic sweord bere   oþðe sidne scyld,
geolorand to guþe,   ac ic mid grape sceal
fon wið feonde   ond ymb feorh sacan,
lað wið laþum;   ðær gelyfan sceal
Dryhtnes dome   se þe hine deað nimeð.
Wen' ic þæt he wille,   gif he wealdan mot,
in þæm guðsele   Geotena leode
etan unforhte,   swa he oft dyde,   [f.142r]
mægenhreð manna.   Na þu minne þearft
hafalan hydan,   ac he me habban wile
d[r]eore fahne,   gif mec deað nimeð;
byreð blodig wæl,   byrgean þenceð,
eteð angenga   unmurnlice,
mearcað morhopu;   nu ðu ymb mines ne þearft
lices feorme   leng sorgian.
Onsend Higelace,   gif mec hild nime,
beaduscruda betst,   þæt mine breost wereð,
hrægla selest;   þæt is Hrædlan laf,
Welandes geweorc.   Gæð a wyrd swa hio scel!'
VII   Hroðgar maþelode,   helm Scyldinga:
'F[o]r [gew]y[r]htum þu,   wine min Beowulf,

stands empty and useless to every warrior,
once the evening-light is hidden
beneath heaven's vault.
So my people, the best wise ceorls,
have advised me thus,
prince Hrothgar, that I should seek thee,
because they knew the power of my strength;
they themselves looked on when I came out of battle,
stained with the blood of foes, where I bound five,
destroyed a race of giants, and on the waves slew
sea-monsters by night; suffered dire distress,
avenged a wrong on the | Weders —sought out woes— [f.141v]
crushed fierce foes; and now against Grendel,
the fierce assailant, I shall settle matters
with that monster alone! So I will now,
lord of the Bright-Danes, protector
of the Scyldings, beg thee one boon,
that thou refuse me not, refuge of warriors,
noble friend, now that I come thus from afar,
that I alone [and] my band of eorls,
this hardy troop of men, may cleanse Heorot.
I have also learned that the fierce assailant
in his rashness cares not for weapons.
Hence —so that Hygelac, my liege lord,
may be well-disposed in mind towards me—
I scorn to bear sword or broad shield,
yellow buckler to battle, but with my grasp
I shall grapple with the fiend and fight for life,
foe against foe; he whom death takes
shall trust in the Lord's judgment there.
I expect that if he is allowed, he will
fearlessly devour the people of the Geats
in the battle-hall, as he has | often done [f.142r]
the flower of men. Thou dost not need
to cover my head, if death takes me,
for he will have me drenched in blood;
he will bear off my bloody corpse, intent on eating it;
the lone-prowler will devour it remorselessly,
staining his moor-retreat; no longer needst thou
be anxious about the sustenance of my body.
Send to Hygelac, if battle takes me,
this best of war-dresses, that defends my breast,
finest of garments; it is Hrethel's heirloom,
Weland's work. Fate ever goes as it must!'

VII Hrothgar spoke, protector of the Scyldings:
'For deeds done in the past, Beowulf my friend,

ond for arstafum   usic sohtest.
Gesloh þin fæder   fæhðe mæste:
wearþ he Heaþolafe   to handbonan
mid Wilfingum;   ða hine [Wede]ra cyn
for herebrogan   habban ne mihte.
Þanon he gesohte   Suð-Dena folc
ofer yða gewealc,   Ar-Scyldinga. [f.142v]
Ða ic furþum weold   folce Den[i]ga
ond on geogoðe heold   gi[nn]e rice,
hordburh hæleþa;   ða wæs Heregar dead,
min yldra mæg   unlifigende,
bearn Healfdenes;   se wæs betera ðonne ic.
Siððan þa fæhðe   feo þingode:
sende ic Wylfingum   ofer wæteres hrycg
ealde madmas;   he me aþas swor.
Sorh is me to secganne   on sefan minum
gumena ængum   hwæt me Grendel hafað
hynðo on Heorote   mid his heteþancum,
færniða gefremed;   is min fletwerod,
wigheap gewanod;   hie wyrd forsweop
on Grendles gryre.   God eaþe mæg
þone dolsceaðan   dæda getwæfan.
Ful oft gebeotedon   beore druncne
ofer ealowæge   oretmecgas,
þæt hie in beorsele   bidan woldon
Grendles guþe   mid gryrum ecga.
Ðonne wæs þeos medoheal   on morgentid,
drihtsele dreorfah   þonne dæg lixte,
eal bencþelu   blode bestymed, [f.143r]
heall heorudreore;   ahte ic holdra þy læs,
deorre duguðe,   þe þa deað fornam.
Site nu to symle,   ond on sæl meoto,
sigehreð secgum,   swa þin sefa hwette.'
   Þa wæs Geatmæcgum   geador ætsomne
on beorsele   benc gerymed;
þær swiðferhþe   sittan eodon,
þryðum dealle.   Þegn nytte beheold,
se þe on handa bær   hroden ealowæge,
scencte scir wered;   scop hwilum sang
hador on Heorote.   Þær wæs hæleða dream,
duguð unlytel   Dena ond Wedera.
VIII [U]nferð maþelode,   Ecglafes bearn,
þe æt fotum sæt   frean Scyldinga,
onband beadurune   —wæs him Beowulfes sið,
modges merefaran,   micel æfþunca,
forþon þe he ne uþe,   þæt ænig oðer man

and for favours thou hast sought us.
Thy father provoked the greatest of feuds:
with his own hand he was the slayer of Heatholaf
among the Wylfings; then the kindred of the Weders
could not keep him for fear of war.
Thence he sought out the people of the South-Danes, | [f.142v]
the Honour-Scyldings, over the sea-swell.
I first ruled the people of the Danes
and in my youth governed a spacious kingdom,
a rich stronghold of warriors; by then Heorogar was dead,
not living, my elder kinsman,
son of Healfdene; he was better than I.
Then I settled the feud with money:
over the sea's back I sent old treasures
to the Wylfings; he swore oaths to me.
It is grief to me in my heart to tell
any man what Grendel has wrought for me
of humiliations in Heorot with his thoughts of hate,
sudden attacks; my hall-troop,
my war-band, is lessened; Fate has swept
them off in Grendel's horror. God can easily
restrain the wild ravager from his deeds.
Full often, drunken with beer,
warriors vowed over the ale-cup
that they would await with dreaded sword-blades
Grendel's attack in the beer-hall.
Then, in the morning, was this mead-hall
blood-stained, when day shone forth,
all the | bench-boards drenched with blood, [f.143r]
the hall with battle-gore; I had the fewer loyal men,
tried warriors, dear to me, since death had carried them off.
Sit down now to the feast, and in due time think
of the glory of victory for men, as thy heart may urge thee.'

Then, for the men of the Geats together,
was a bench cleared in the beer-hall;
thither went the stout-hearted ones to sit,
proud in their strength. A thane performed his duty,
who bore in his hands an adorned ale-cup,
poured the bright, sweet drink; at times a scop sang
clear in Heorot. There was joy of heroes,
no small body of retainers, Danes and Weders.

VIII Unferth spoke, son of Ecglaf,
who sat at the feet of the lord of the Scyldings,
began a dispute —the venture of Beowulf,
the brave seafarer, was a great bitterness to him,
because he would not grant that any other man

æfre | mærða þon ma   middangeardes   [f.143v]
gehedde under heofenum   þonne he sylfa:
'Eart þu se Beowulf   se þe wið Brecan wunne,
on sidne sæ   ymb sund flite?
Ðær git for wlence   wada cunnedon,
ond for dolgilpe   on deop wæter
aldrum neþdon;   ne inc ænig mon,
ne leof ne lað,   belean mihte
sorhfullne sið   þa git on sund reon.
Þær git eagorstream   earmum þehton,
mæton merestræta,   mundum brugdon,
glidon ofer garsecg.   Geofon yþum weol,
wintrys wylm[um];   git on wæteres æht
seofon niht swuncon.   He þe æt sunde oferflat,
hæfde mare mægen.   Þa hine on morgentid
on Heaþo-Ræmes   holm up ætbær;
ðonon he gesohte   swæsne eðel,
leof his leodum,   lond Brondinga,
freoðoburh fægere   þær he folc ahte,
burh ond beagas. | Beot eal wið þe   [f.144r]
sunu Beanstanes   soðe gelæste.
Ðonne wene ic to þe   wyrsan geþingea,
ðeah þu heaðoræsa   gehwær dohte,
grimre guðe,   gif þu Grendles dearst
nihtlongne fyrst   nean bidan.'
Beowulf maþelode,   bearn Ecgþeowes:
'Hwæt, þu worn fela,   wine min [U]nferð,
beore druncen   ymb Brecan spræce,
sægdest from his siðe!   Soð ic talige,
þæt ic merestrengo   maran ahte,
earfeþo on yþum,   ðonne ænig oþer man.
Wit þæt gecwædon   cnihtwesende
ond gebeotedon   —wæron begen þa git
on geogoðfeore—   þæt wit on garsecg ut
aldrum neðdon,   ond þæt geæfndon swa.
Hæfdon swurd nacod   þa wit on sund reon,
heard on handa;   wit unc wið hronfixas
werian þohton.   No he wiht fram me
flodyþum feor   fleotan meahte,
hraþor on holme;   no ic fram him wolde.
Ða wit æt|somne   on sæ wæron   [f.145v]
fif nihta fyrst   oþþæt unc flod todraf,
wado weallende,   wedera cealdost,
nipende niht,   ond norþanwind
heaðogrim ondhwearf;   hreo wæron yþa.
Wæs merefixa   mod onhrered;

on earth should, beneath the heavens, care more about [f.143v]
glorious deeds than he himself did.
'Art thou that Beowulf who strove with Breca,
competed at swimming in the open sea?
There ye two for pride tackled the waters,
and ventured your lives in deep water
for a foolish boast; nor could any man,
friend or foe, dissuade you two
from the perilous venture, when ye went swimming.
There ye two covered the sea-currents with your arms,
traversed the sea-ways, thrashed with your hands,
glided over the ocean. The sea surged with waves,
winter's welling; ye two in the water's power
toiled seven nights. He overcame thee in swimming,
had more strength. Then in the morning
the sea carried him to the land of the Heatho-Ræmas;
thence he sought his beloved homeland,
dear to his people, the land of the Brondings,
the fair stronghold, where he possessed folk,
stronghold and rings. | All his boast with thee [f.144r]
the son of Beanstan faithfully fulfilled.
Wherefore I expect a worse outcome from thee,
though everywhere thou hast prevailed in battle-storms,
grim warfare, if thou durst await Grendel
at close quarters for the space of a night.'
Beowulf spoke, son of Ecgtheow:
'Well, my friend Unferth, thou hast spoken a great deal
about Breca, drunken with beer,
told about his venture! I maintain the truth
that I had more strength in the sea,
hardships in the waves, than any other man.
As youths, we two agreed
and vowed —we were both then still
in our boyhood— that we two would venture our lives
on the ocean, and that we did accordingly.
When we two swam in the sea we held naked swords,
boldly in our hands; we thought to protect ourselves
against whales. Not at all could he
float far from me on the sea-waves,
swifter on the sea; I had no wish to abandon him.
Thus we two were to|gether in the sea [f.144v]
for the space of five nights until the flood drove us apart,
the surge of waters, coldest of weathers,
darkening night, and a biting wind from the north
turned against us; rough were the waves.
Aroused was the anger of the sea-fish;

þær me wið laðum licsyrce min,
heard hondlocen, helpe gefremede,
beadohrægl broden on breostum læg,
golde gegyrwed. Me to grunde teah
fah feondscaða, fæste hæfde
grim on grape; hwæþre me gyfeþe wearð
þæt ic aglæcan orde geræhte,
hildebille; heaþoræs fornam
mihtig meredeor þurh mine hand.
VIIII Swa mec gelome laðgeteonan
þreatedon þearle. Ic him þenode
deoran sweorde, swa hit gedefe wæs.
Næs hie ðære fylle gefean hæfdon,
manfordædlan, þæt hie me þegon,
symbel ymbsæton sægrunde neah;
ac on mergenne mecum wunde [f.145r]
be yðlafe uppe lægon,
sweo[r]dum aswefede, þæt syðþan na
ymb brontne ford brimliðende
lade ne letton. Leoht eastan com,
beorht beacen Godes; brimu swaþredon,
þæt ic sænæssas geseon mihte,
windige weallas. Wyrd oft nereð
unfægne eorl þonne his ellen deah!
Hwæþere me gesælde þæt ic mid sweorde ofsloh
niceras nigene. No ic on niht gefrægn
under heofones hwealf heardran feohtan
ne on egstreamum earmran mannon;
hw[æ]þere ic fara feng feore gedigde,
siþes werig. Ða mec sæ oþbær,
flod æfter faroðe, on Finna land,
w[a]du weallendu. No ic wiht fram þe
swylcra searoniða secgan hyrde,
billa brogan. Breca næfre git
æt heaðolace, ne gehwæþer incer,
swa deorlice dæd gefremede
fagum sweordum (no ic þæs [fela] gylpe),
þeah ðu þinum broðrum to banan wurde,
heafodmægum; þæs þu in helle scealt [f.145v]
werhðo dreogan, þeah þin wit duge.
Secge ic þe to soðe, sunu Ecglafes,
þæt næfre Gre[n]del swa fela gryra gefremede,
atol æglæca, ealdre þinum,
hynðo on Heorote, gif þin hige wære,
sefa swa searogrim, swa þu self talast.
Ac he hafað onfunden þæt he þa fæhðe ne þearf,

there my mail-shirt, hard and hand-linked,
furnished me help against foes;
the woven battle-garment, gold-adorned,
covered my breast. A deadly destructive foe
dragged me to the bottom, held me firmly,
grim in his grip; but it was granted me
to pierce the fierce assailant with my sword-point,
my battle-sword; the battle-storm destroyed
the mighty sea-beast by my hand.
VIIII Thus often the hateful ravagers
harrassed me severely. With my good sword
I served them as it was fitting.
By no means did those evil-doers have joy
of that feast, of consuming me,
sitting round a banquet by the bottom of the sea;
but in the morning | wounded with swords, [f.145r]
they lay up along the shore,
slain by swords, so that thereafter
they would never hinder the passage of seafarers
across the high sea. Light came from the east,
God's bright beacon; the sea grew calm,
so that I could see headlands,
wind-swept cliffs. Fate often saves
an undoomed man, when his valour avails!
Yet it was granted me that I slew with my sword
nine water-monsters! Never have I heard
of a harder fight at night under heaven's vault,
nor of a man more wretched in the sea-streams;
yet I escaped with my life the grasp of foes,
weary of my venture. Then the sea carried me off,
the flood on its current, the surging waters,
to the land of the Lapps. I have never heard
such skilful contests, terror of swords,
recounted of thee. Never yet did Breca
at the battle-play, nor either of you two,
accomplish so bold a deed
with shining swords (I boast not [much] of it),
though thou didst become thy brothers' slayer,
thy close kinsmen; for that thou shalt in | hell [f.145v]
suffer damnation, even though thy wit be keen.
I tell thee truly, son of Ecglaf,
that Grendel, the terrible, fierce assailant, would never
have accomplished so many horrors against thy lord,
humiliations in Heorot, if thy heart,
thy spirit, had been so fierce in battle as thou sayest thyself.
But he has found out that he need not greatly

atole ecgþræce   eower leode
swiðe onsittan,   Sige-Scyldinga;
nymeð nydbade,   nænegum arað
leode Deniga,   ac he lust wigeð,
swefeð ond sendeþ,   secce ne weneþ
to Gar-Denum.   Ac ic him Geata sceal
eafoð ond ellen   ungeara nu,
guþe gebeodan.   Gæþ eft se þe mot
to medo modig,   siþþan morgenleoht
ofer ylda bearn   oþres dogores,
sunne sweglwered   suþan scineð!'
   Þa wæs on salum   sinces brytta,
gamolfeax ond guðrof;   geoce gelyfde
brego Beorht-Dena;   gehyrde on Beowulfe   [f.146r]
folces hyrde   fæstrædne geþoht.
   Ðær wæs hæleþa hleahtor,   hlyn swynsode,
word wæron wynsume.   Eode Wealhþeow forð,
cwen Hroðgares   cynna gemyndig,
grette goldhroden   guman on healle,
ond þa freolic wif   ful gesealde
ærest East-Dena   eþelwearde,
bæd hine bliðne   æt þære beorþege,
leodum leofne;   he on lust geþeah
symbel ond seleful,   sigerof kyning.
Ymbeode þa   ides Helminga
duguþe ond geogoþe   dæl æghwylcne,
sincfato sealde,   oþþæt sæl alamp,
þæt hio Beowulfe,   beaghroden cwen
mode geþungen   medoful ætbær.
Grette Geata leod,   Gode þancode
wisfæst wordum   þæs ðe hire se willa gelamp,
þæt heo on ænigne   eorl gelyfde
fyrena frofre.   He þæt ful geþeah,
wælreow wiga   æt Wealhþeon,   [f.146v]
ond þa gyddode   guþe gefysed,
Beowulf maþelode,   bearn Ecgþeowes:
'Ic þæt hogode,   þa ic on holm gestah,
sæbat gesæt   mid minra secga gedriht,
þæt ic anunga   eowra leoda
willan geworhte,   oþðe on wæl crunge
feondgrapum fæst.   Ic gefremman sceal
eorlic ellen,   oþðe endedæg
on þisse meoduhealle   minne gebidan!'
Ðam wife þa word   wel licodon,
gilpcwide Geates;   eode goldhroden
freolicu folccwen   to hire frean sittan.

fear hostility, a terrible sword-storm
from your people, the Victory-Scyldings;
he takes enforced toll, shows mercy to none
of the people of the Danes, but he takes pleasure,
kills and despatches, expects no conflict
from the Spear-Danes. But soon now I shall
show him the strength and courage of the Geats
in battle. Afterwards, he who may shall go
boldly to the mead, when the morning-light
of another day, the sun clothed in radiance,
shines from the south over the sons of men!'
Then glad was the treasure-giver,
grey-haired and battle-brave; the | prince of the Bright- [f.146r]
Danes counted on help; the protector of the people
heard in Beowulf a resolute purpose.
There was laughter of warriors, noise resounded,
words were winsome. Wealhtheow went forth,
Hrothgar's queen, mindful of courtesy,
gold-adorned, greeted the men in hall,
and then the noble lady gave the goblet first
to the guardian of the land of the East-Danes,
bade him be joyful at the beer-drinking,
dear to his people; he, victorious king,
partook of feast and hall-cup with pleasure.
Then the lady of the Helmings went round
everywhere, among old and young warriors,
proffered precious cups, until the time came
that she, ring-adorned queen, excellent of mind,
carried the mead-cup to Beowulf.
She greeted the man of the Geats, thanked God
for the fact that her wish had been fulfilled,
that she might count on some eorl
for relief from wicked deeds. He, the warrior
fierce in battle, received the cup | from Wealhtheow, [f.146v]
and then spoke, eager for battle;
Beowulf spoke, son of Ecgtheow:
'I resolved, when I set out on the sea,
sat in the sea-boat with my company of men,
that I would fulfil completely
the wish of your people, or fall in death,
held fast in the enemy's grasp. I shall accomplish
a heroic deed of courage, or experience
my last day in this mead-hall!'
These words pleased the lady well,
the Geat's vaunting speech; adorned with gold,
the noble queen of the people went to sit by her lord.

Þa wæs eft swa ær   inne on healle
þryðword sprecen,   ðeod on sælum,
sigefolca sweg,   oþþæt semninga
sunu Healfdenes   secean wolde
æfenræste;   wiste þæm ahlæcan
to þæm heahsele   hilde geþinged,
siððan hie sunnan leoht   geseon meahton,
oþðe nipende   niht ofer ealle,
scaduhelma gesceapu   scriðan cwoman
wan under wolcnum.   Werod eall aras.
[Ge]grette þa   guma oþerne,
Hroðgar Beowulf,   ond him hæl abead,
winærnes geweald,   ond þæt word acwæð: [f.147r]
'Næfre ic ænegum men   ær alyfde,
siþðan ic hond ond rond   hebban mihte,
ðryþærn Dena   buton þe nu ða.
Hafa nu ond geheald   husa selest,
gemyne mærþo,   mægenellen cyð,
waca wið wraþum!   Ne bið þe wilna gad
gif þu þæt ellenweorc   aldre gedigest.'
X   Ða him Hroþgar gewat   mid his hæleþa gedryht,
eodur Scyldinga   ut of healle;
wolde wigfruma   Wealhþeo secan,
cwen to gebeddan.   Hæfde Kyningwuldor
Grendle togeanes,   swa guman gefrungon,
seleweard aseted;   sundornytte beheold
ymb aldor Dena,   eotonweard' abead.
Huru Geata leod   georne truwode
modgan mægnes,   Metodes hyldo.
Ða he him of dyde   isernbyrnan,
helm of hafelan,   sealde his hyrsted sweord,
irena cyst   ombihtþegne,
ond gehealdan het   hildegeatwe.
Gespræc þa se goda   gylpworda sum,
Beowulf Geata,   ær he on bed stige: [f.147v]
'No ic me an herewæsmun   hnagran talige,
guþgeweorca,   þonne Grendel hine;
forþan ic hine sweorde   swebban nelle,
aldre beneotan,   þeah ic eal mæge;
nat he þara goda,   þæt he me ongean slea,
rand geheawe,   þeah ðe he rof sie
niþgeweorca;   ac wit on niht sculon
secge ofersittan,   gif h[e] gesecean dear
wig ofer wæpen,   ond siþðan witig God
on swa hwæþere hond,   halig Dryhten,
mærðo deme   swa him gemet þince!'

Then again, as before, were brave words spoken
in the hall, the people in happiness,
the sound of victorious people, till soon
the son of Healfdene wished to go to his night's rest;
he knew that a battle had been planned
for the fierce assailant in the lofty hall,
after they could not see the light of the sun,
and darkening night came over all,
when shadowy shapes came stalking,
dark beneath the clouds. The whole company rose.
Then one warrior greeted the other,
Hrothgar Beowulf, and wished him success, | [f.147r]
control of the wine-hall, and uttered these words:
'Never before, since I could raise hand and shield,
have I entrusted the mighty hall of the Danes
to any man, except now to thee.
Keep now and protect this best of houses:
think of thy fame, show mighty courage,
watch against foes! Nor shalt thou lack desirable things
if thou survivest that courageous deed with thy life.'
X Then Hrothgar, protector of the Scyldings,
went out of the hall with his band of warriors;
the war-leader wished to go to Wealhtheow,
his queen, as consort. The King of glory had,
so men had learned, appointed a hall-guard
against Grendel, who fulfilled a special service
towards the lord of the Danes, guarded against a giant.
Indeed the man of the Geats trusted firmly
in his fearless strength, and the favour of the Creator.
Then he removed his iron byrny,
the helmet from his head, gave his decorated sword,
best of blades, to the attendant thane,
and ordered him to guard his war-gear.
Then the valiant one, Beowulf of the | Geats, [f.147v]
uttered some vaunting words, ere he lay down on his bed:
'I count myself no poorer in war-strength,
in battle-deeds, than Grendel does himself;
wherefore, I do not wish to slay him with a sword,
deprive him of life, though surely I might;
he knows naught of these skills, that he may strike at me,
hew my shield, mighty though he be
in hostile deeds; but we two at night
shall forgo swords, if he dares to seek
battle without arms, and then may the wise God,
the holy Lord, decree glory
to whichever side seems meet to him!'

Hylde hine þa heaþodeor, hleorbolster onfeng
eorles andwlitan, ond hine ymb monig
snellic særinc selereste gebeah.
Nænig heora þohte þæt he þanon scolde
eft eardlufan æfre gesecean,
folc oþðe freoburh þær he afeded wæs;
ac hie hæfdon gefrunen þæt hie ær to fela micles
in þæm winsele wældeað fornam,
Denigea leode. Ac him Dryhten forgeaf
wigspeda gewiofu, Wedera leodum [f.148r]
frofor ond fultum, þæt hie feond heora
ðurh anes cræft ealle ofercomon,
selfes mihtum. Soð is gecyþed,
þæt mihtig God manna cynnes
weold [w]ideferhð.
Com on wanre niht
scriðan sceadugenga. Sceotend swæfon,
þa þæt hornreced healdan scoldon,
ealle buton anum. Þæt wæs yldum cuþ,
þæt hie ne moste, þa Metod nolde,
se s[c]ynscaþa, under sceadu bregdan;
ac he wæccende wraþum on andan
bad bolgenmod beadwa geþinges.

XI Ða com of more under misthleoþum
Grendel gongan, Godes yrre bær;
mynte se manscaða manna cynnes
sumne besyrwan in sele þam hean.
Wod under wolcnum to þæs þe he winreced,
goldsele gumena gearwost wisse,
fættum fahne. Ne wæs þæt forma sið,
þæt he Hroþgares ham gesohte;
næfre he on aldordagum ær ne siþðan [f.148v]
heardran hæle healðegnas fand.
Com þa to recede rinc siðian,
dreamum bedæled. Duru sona onarn,
fyrbendum fæst, syþðan he hire folmum [g]*e*hran;
onbræd þa bealohydig, ða [he ge]bolgen wæs,
recedes muþan. Raþe æfter þon
on fagne flor feond treddode,
eode yrremod; him of eagum stod
ligge gelicost leoht unfæger.
Geseah he in recede rinca manige,
swefan sibbegedriht samod ætgædere,
magorinca heap. Þa his mod ahlog;
mynte þæt he gedælde, ærþon dæg cwome,
atol aglæca, anra gehwylces

The battle-brave one lay down, the bolster received
the eorl's face, and around him many
a brave seaman lay down on his bed in hall.
None of them thought that he should go thence,
ever again reach his beloved homeland,
folk or noble stronghold where he was brought up;
but they had learned that deadly slaughter had previously
carried off far too many of the Danish people,
in that wine-hall. But to the people of the | Weders [f.148r]
the Lord granted the fortune of success in war,
comfort and aid, that they all overcame
their enemy through the power of one man,
his own might. The truth is well-known
that almighty God has for ever ruled
over mankind.
In the dark night came
stalking the walker in shadows. The warriors slept,
who had to guard that gabled hall,
all except one. That was known to men
that when the Creator willed it not,
the demonic ravager was not allowed to drag them
beneath the shadows; but he, watching for foes,
awaited enraged the outcome of the fight.

XI

Then came Grendel, advancing from the moor
beneath the misty slopes; he bore God's wrath;
the wicked ravager intended to ensnare
one of the race of men in the lofty hall.
Beneath the clouds he advanced to where he discerned
the wine-hall most clearly, the gold-hall of men,
gleaming with gold plating. Nor was that the first time
that he had come to Hrothgar's home;
never before | or since in the days of his life [f.148v]
did he find hall-thanes with worse fortune.
Then the warrior came making his way to the hall,
deprived of joys. Soon the door, firm with forged bars,
sprang open, when he touched it with his hands;
bent on destruction, for he was enraged,
he tore open the hall-door. Quickly after that
the fiend stepped on to the decorated floor,
advanced angrily; in his eyes gleamed
an ugly light, most like a flame.
He saw many warriors in the hall,
a band of kinsmen sleeping together,
a troop of young warriors. Then his heart exulted;
the fierce assailant intended ere day came
to sever the life of each one

lif wið lice, þa him alumpen wæs
wistfylle wen. Ne wæs þæt wyrd þa gen,
þæt he ma moste manna cynnes
ðicgean ofer þa niht. Þryðswyð beheold
mæg Higelaces, hu se manscaða
under færgripum gefaran wolde.
Ne þæt se aglæca yldan þohte,
ac he gefeng hraðe forman siðe [f.149r]
slæpendne rinc, slat unwearnum,
bat banlocan, blod edrum dranc,
synsnædum swealh; sona hæfde
unlyfigendes eal gefeormod,
fet ond folma. Forð near ætstop,
nam þa mid handa higeþihtigne
rinc on ræste, ræhte ongean
feond mid folme; he onfeng hraþe
inwitþancum ond wið earm gesæt.
Sona þæt onfunde fyrena hyrde,
þæt he ne mette middangeardes,
eorþan scea[t]a on elran men
mundgripe maran; he on mode wearð
forht on ferhðe; no þy ær fram meahte.
Hyge wæs him hinfus, wolde on heolster fleon,
secan deofla gedræg; ne wæs his drohtað þær
swylce he on ealderdagum ær gemette.
Gemunde þa se [m]od[g]a mæg Higelaces
æfenspræce, uplang astod
ond him fæste wiðfeng; fingras burston;
eoten wæs utweard, eorl furþur stop.
Mynte se mæra, [þ]ær he meahte swa, [f.149v]
widre gewindan ond on weg þanon
fleon on fenhopu; wiste his fingra geweald
on grames grapum. Þæt wæs geocor sið,
þæt se hearmscaþa to Heorute ateah!
Dryhtsele dynede; Denum eallum wearð,
ceasterbuendum, cenra gehwylcum,
eorlum ealuscerwen. Yrre wæron begen,
reþe renweardas; reced hlynsode.
Þa wæs wundor micel þæt se winsele
wiðhæfde heaþodeorum, þæt he on hrusan ne feol,
fæger foldbold; ac he þæs fæste wæs
innan ond utan irenbendum
searoþoncum besmiþod. Þær fram sylle abeag
medubenc monig, mine gefræge,
golde geregnad, þær þa graman wunnon.
Þæs ne wendon ær witan Scyldinga,

from his body, for the hope of feasting full
had come to him. It was no longer destined that he
would be permitted to take more of mankind
after that night. The mighty kinsman of Hygelac
watched how the wicked ravager
would proceed with his sudden attack.
The fierce assailant was not minded to delay,
but he quickly | seized a sleeping warrior [f.149r]
at the first opportunity, rent him ravenously,
bit his muscle, drank blood from his veins,
swallowed sinful morsels; soon he had
consumed all of the dead man,
feet and hands. Forward and nearer he stepped,
then with his hands grasped the strong-hearted
warrior on his bed; the fiend reached out
towards him with his hand; he quickly seized him
with hostile intent and sat up leaning on his arm.
At once the master of wicked deeds found out
that never in the world, in the regions of the earth,
had he met with a mightier hand-grip
in another man; he became afraid in mind
and spirit; yet none the sooner could he escape.
He was minded to get away, flee into darkness,
seek his swarm of devils; what he found there was not
such as he had met with before in the days of his life.
Then the brave kinsman of Hygelac remembered
his evening's speech; he stood upright
and grasped him firmly; his fingers cracked;
the giant was striving to escape, the eorl stepped forward.
The infamous one intended to escape farther off, | [f.149v]
wherever he could, and flee thence
to his fen-retreat; he knew the power of his fingers
was in a hostile grasp. That was a bitter journey
that the grievous ravager undertook to Heorot!
The noble hall resounded; in all the Danes,
fortress-dwellers, each of the brave men,
eorls, there was fear. Both were furious,
fierce hall-guardians; the hall resounded.
Then was it great wonder that the wine-hall
withstood the brave fighters, that the fair building
did not fall to the ground; but it was firmly fixed
within and without with iron bands
skilfully forged. There started away from the floor,
as I have heard, many a mead-bench,
gold-adorned, where the foemen fought.
Before that, the wise men of the Scyldings

þæt hit a mid gemete   manna ænig
[b]etlic ond banfag   tobrecan meahte,
listum tolucan,   nymþe liges fæþm
swulge on swaþule.   Sweg up astag [f.150r]
niwe geneahhe;   Norð-Denum stod
atelic egesa,   anra gehwylcum
þara þe of wealle   wop gehyrdon,
gryreleoð galan   Godes andsacan,
sigeleasne sang,   sar wanigean
helle hæfton.   Heold hine fæste
se þe manna wæs   mægene strengest
on þæm dæge   þysses lifes.

XII Nolde eorla hleo   ænige þinga
þone cwealmcuman   cwicne forlætan,
ne his lifdagas   leoda ænigum
nytte tealde.   Þær genehost brægd
eorl Beowulfes   ealde lafe,
wolde freadrihtnes   feorh ealgian,
mæres þeodnes,   ðær hie meahton swa.
Hie þæt ne wiston,   þa hie gewin drugon,
heardhicgende   hildemecgas,
ond on healfa gehwone   heawan þohton,
sawle secan: þone synscaðan
ænig ofer eorþan   irenna cyst,
guðbilla nan   gretan nolde;
ac he sigewæpnum   forsworen hæfde, [f.150v]
ecga gehwylcre.   Scolde his aldorgedal
on ðæm dæge   þysses lifes
earmlic wurðan,   ond se ellorgast
on feonda geweald   feor siðian.
   Ða þæt onfunde   se þe fela æror
modes myrðe   manna cynne,
fyrene gefremede   —he fag wið God—
þæt him se lichoma   læstan nolde,
ac hine se modega   mæg Hygelaces
hæfde be honda;   wæs gehwæþer oðrum
lifigende lað.   Licsar gebad
atol æglæca;   him on eaxle wearð
syndolh sweotol,   seonowe onsprungon,
burston banlocan.   Beowulfe wearð
guðhreð gyfeþe;   scolde Grendel þonan
feorhseoc fleon   under fenhleoðu,
secean wynleas wic;   wiste þe geornor,
þæt his aldres wæs   ende gegongen,
dogera dægrim.   Denum eallum wearð
æfter þam wælræse   willa gelumpen.

thought that no man could ever shatter it,
splendid and bone-adorned, rend it with malice
in any way, unless the embrace of fire
should swallow it in flame. A sound | arose, [f.150r]
often new; a terrible fear
came upon the North-Danes, upon every one
of those who heard the wailing from the wall,
God's adversary sounding a chant of terror,
a song of defeat, the captive of hell lamenting
his wound. He held him fast
who of men was strongest in might
at that time in this life.

XII The protector of eorls would not by any means
let the deadly visitant escape alive,
nor did he consider the days of Grendel's life
of use to any man. There many of Beowulf's
eorls brandished ancient ancestral swords,
wished to protect the life of their lord,
the famous prince, if only they could.
They knew not, brave-minded warriors,
when they engaged in the conflict,
and thought to strike him on every side,
to seek out his soul, that no war-sword
on earth, the finest of blades,
would touch the evil ravager;
for he had | renounced weapons of victory, [f.150v]
every blade. His severing from life
at that time was doomed
to be wretched, and the alien spirit
was to travel far into the power of fiends.
Then he who had formerly carried out
upon mankind many afflictions of the heart,
wicked deeds —he (being) at feud with God—
found that his body would not be of service,
but the courageous kinsman of Hygelac
had him by the hand; each was hateful
to the other while he lived. The fierce assailant
suffered bodily pain; on his shoulder was visible
an incurable wound, sinews sprang apart,
muscles burst. Beowulf was granted
triumph in battle; Grendel had thence to flee
under fenland-slopes mortally wounded,
seek out his joyless dwelling; he knew the more surely
that his life's end was reached,
the number of his days. For all the Danes
was their desire fulfilled after the deadly onslaught.

Hæfde þa gefælsod se þe ær feorran com,
snotor ond swyðferhð, sele Hroðgares,
genered wið niðe; nihtweorce gefeh, [f.151r]
ellenmærþum. Hæfde East-Denum
Geatmecga leod gilp gelæsted,
swylce oncyþðe ealle gebette,
inwidsorge þe hie ær drugon
ond for þreanydum þolian scoldon,
torn unlytel. Þæt wæs tacen sweotol,
syþðan hildedeor hond alegde,
earm ond eaxle —þær wæs eal geador
Grendles grape— under geapne hr[of].

XIII Đa wæs on morgen, mine gefræge,
ymb þa gifhealle guðrinc monig;
ferdon folctogan feorran ond nean
geond widwegas wundor sceawian,
laþes lastas. No his lifgedal
sarlic þuhte secga ænegum
þara þe tirleases trode sceawode,
hu he werigmod on weg þanon,
niða ofercumen, on nicera mere
fæge ond geflymed feorhlastas bær.
Đær wæs on blode brim weallende,
atol yða geswing eal gemenged,
haton heolfre, heorodreore weol; [f.151v]
deaðfæge deog siððan dreama leas
in fenfreoðo feorh alegde,
hæþene sawle; þær him hel onfeng.
   Þanon eft gewiton ealdgesiðas,
swylce geong manig of gomenwaþe,
fram mere modge mearum ridan,
beornas on blancum. Đær wæs Beowulfes
mærðo mæned; monig oft gecwæð,
þætte suð ne norð be sæm tweonum
ofer eormengrund oþer nænig
under swegles begong selra nære
rondhæbbendra, rices wyrðra
—ne hie huru winedrihten wiht ne logon,
glædne Hroðgar, ac þæt wæs god cyning.
Hwilum heaþorofe hleapan leton,
on geflit faran fealwe mearas
ðær him foldwegas fægere þuhton,
cystum cuðe. Hwilum cyninges þegn,
guma gilphlæden, gidda gemyndig,
se ðe ealfela ealdgesegena
worn gemunde, word oþer fand

Thus had he who first came from afar,
wise and resolute, cleansed Hrothgar's hall,
saved it from | affliction; rejoiced in his night's work, [f.151r]
heroic deeds. The man of the Geats
had fulfilled his pledge to the East-Danes;
so too, had he made good all grief,
evil sorrow which they endured formerly
and had to suffer from dire need,
no little distress. That was a clear sign
when the battle-brave man placed the hand,
arm and shoulder —there was all
of Grendel's grasp— under the broad roof.

XIII Then, in the morning, as I have heard,
there was many a warrior around the gift-hall;
leaders of the people came from far and near
through distant regions to examine that marvel,
the tracks of the foe. His severing from life
seemed not painful to any man
who looked at the footprints of the inglorious one,
how he, weary-hearted, went from there,
defeated in battle, doomed and put to flight,
bore life-tracks to the water-monsters' mere.
There was the water boiling with blood,
the terrible swirl of the waves all mingled
with hot gore, surging with sword | -blood; [f.151v]
doomed to die he had hidden, then, deprived
of joys, laid down his life, his heathen soul,
in his fen-refuge; there hell received him.
  From there the old retainers turned back,
also many a young man, from the joyous journey,
to ride from the mere, high-spirited on horses,
warriors on steeds. There was Beowulf's
glory related; many often said
that, south or north, between the seas,
over the spacious earth no other man
beneath the sky's expanse was better
among shield-bearers, more worthy of a kingdom
—yet they found no fault at all with their friend and lord,
the gracious Hrothgar, for he was a good king.
At times the battle-brave men allowed
their bay horses to gallop, to race
where the paths seemed attractive,
known for their excellence. At times a king's thane,
a man filled with eloquence, recalling stories,
he who recalled a great many traditional tales,
a multitude, devised another in words

soðe gebunden;   secg eft ongan
sið Beowulfes   snyttrum styrian,   [f.152r]
ond on sped wrecan   spel gerade,
wordum wrixlan.   Welhwylc gecwæð
þæt he fram Sigemunde[s]   secgan hyrde
ellendædum,   uncuþes fela,
Wælsinges gewin,   wide siðas,
þara þe gumena bearn   gearwe ne wiston,
fæhðe ond fyrena,   buton Fitela mid hine,
þonne he swulces hwæt   secgan wolde,
eam his nefan,   swa hie a wæron
æt niða gehwam   nydgesteallan;
hæfdon ealfela   eotena cynnes
sweordum gesægd.   Sigemunde gesprong
æfter deaðdæge   dom unlytel,
syþðan wiges heard   wyrm acwealde,
hordes hyrde;   he under harne stan,
æþelinges bearn   ana geneðde
frecne dæde,   ne wæs him Fitela mid;
hwæþre him gesælde   ðæt þæt swurd þurhwod
wrætlicne wyrm   þæt hit on wealle ætstod,
dryhtlic iren;   draca morðre swealt.
Hæfde aglæca   elne gegongen
þæt he beahhordes   brucan moste
selfes dome; | sæbat gehleod,   [f.152v]
bær on bearm scipes   beorhte frætwa
Wælses eafera;   wyrm hat gemealt.
  Se wæs wreccena   wide mærost
ofer werþeode,   wigendra hleo,
ellendædum   —he þæs ær onðah—
siððan Heremodes   hild sweðrode,
e[a]foð ond ellen.   He mid Eotenum wearð
on feonda geweald   forð forlacen,
snude forsended.   Hine sorhwylmas
lemede to lange;   he his leodum wearð,
eallum æþellingum   to aldorceare;
swylce oft bemearn   ærran mælum
swiðferhþes sið   snotor ceorl monig,
se þe him bealwa to   bote gelyfde,
þæt þæt ðeodnes bearn   geþeon scolde,
fæderæþelum onfon,   folc gehealdan,
hord ond hleoburh,   hæleþa rice,
eþel Scyldinga.   He þær eallum wearð,
mæg Higelaces   manna cynne,
freondum gefægra;   hine fyren onwod.
  Hwilum flitende   fealwe stræte

correctly linked; the man proceeded
with skill to recount Beowulf's exploit,
and recite with success a skilful tale,
varying his words. He related everything [f.152r]
that he had heard said of Sigemund's
many unknown deeds of courage,
the Wælsing's conflict, wide wanderings,
of which the sons of men knew naught,
feuds and wicked deeds, except for Fitela
(who was) with him when he would tell all,
the uncle to his nephew, for they ever were
comrades in need in every struggle;
a great many of the race of giants had they
laid low with swords. For Sigemund
after his death-day earned no little fame,
when, battle-hard, he killed the serpent,
guardian of the hoard; beneath the grey stone,
the prince's son, had ventured alone,
on a daring deed; Fitela was not with him;
yet it befell him that that sword went through
the wondrous serpent, so that the lordly sword
stood fast in the wall; the dragon died violently.
The fierce warrior had brought about by his valour
that he was able to enjoy the ring-hoard,
at his own will; | the son of Wæls loaded [f.152v]
the sea-boat, bore bright treasures into
the ship's bosom; the hot serpent melted away.
  He, the protector of warriors, was by far
the most famous of exiles among nations,
for deeds of courage —he had prospered from that—
after Heremod's prowess in war had diminished,
his strength and valour. He among the Jutes
was betrayed into the power of his enemies,
quickly put to death. Surging sorrows
oppressed him too long; to his people, he became
a great anxiety, to all his noblemen;
also many a wise ceorl in earlier times
often lamented the valiant one's way of life,
who had counted on him for relief from their afflictions,
that that prince's son might prosper,
receive his father's rank, rule over the people,
treasure and stronghold, the realm of heroes,
the homeland of the Scyldings. He, the kinsman
of Hygelac, there became dearer to his friends
and to all mankind; sin entered Heremod's heart.
  Sometimes racing their horses they traversed

mearum mæton. Đa wæs morgenleoht
scofen ond scynded. Eode scealc monig [f.153r]
swiðhicgende to sele þam hean
searowundor seon; swylce self cyning
of brydbure, beahhorda weard,
tryddode tirfæst getrume micle,
cystum gecyþed, ond his cwen mid him
medostigge mæt mægþa hose.
XIIII Hroðgar maþelode —he to healle geong,
stod on staþole, geseah steapne hrof
golde fahne ond Grendles hond:
'Đisse ansyne Alwealdan þanc
lungre gelimpe! Fela ic laþes gebad,
grynna æt Grendle; a mæg God wyrcan
wunder æfter wundre, wuldres Hyrde.
Đæt wæs ungeara þæt ic ænigra me
weana ne wende to widan feore
bote gebidan, þonne blode fah
husa selest heorodreorig stod,
wea widscofen witena gehwylc[um]
ðara þe ne wendon, þæt hie wideferhð
leoda landgeweorc laþum beweredon
scuccum ond scinnum. Nu scealc hafað [f.153v]
þurh Drihtnes miht dæd gefremede
ðe we ealle ær ne meahton
snyttrum besyrwan. Hwæt, þæt secgan mæg
efne swa hwylc mægþa swa ðone magan cende
æfter gumcynnum, gyf heo gyt lyfað,
þæt hyre Ealdmetod este wære
bearngebyrdo. Nu ic, Beowulf, þec,
secg betsta, me for sunu wylle
freogan on ferhþe; heald forð tela
niwe sibbe. Ne bið þe [n]ænigre gad
worolde wilna, þe ic geweald hæbbe.
Ful oft ic for læssan lean teohhode,
hordweorþunge hnahran rince,
sæmran æt sæcce. Þu þe self hafast
dædum gefremed, þæt þin [dom] lyfað
awa to aldre. Alwalda þec
gode forgylde, swa he nu gyt dyde!'
Beowulf maþelode, bearn Ec[g]þeowes:
'We þæt ellenweorc estum miclum,
feohtan fremedon, frecne geneðdon
eafoð uncuþes. Uþe ic swiþor,
þæt ðu hine selfne geseon moste,
feond on frætewum fylwerigne!

the tawny roads. Then had the morning-light
advanced, hastening on. | Many a retainer went, [f.153r]
resolute in mind, to the high hall
to look at the strange wonder; also the king himself
from his bed-chamber, guardian of ring-hoards,
stepped glorious with a great troop,
renowned for his virtues, and his queen with him
traversed the path to the mead-hall with her troop of maidens.

XIIII Hrothgar spoke —he went to the hall,
stood on the steps, gazed at the lofty roof
gleaming with gold and Grendel's hand—:
'For this sight may thanks be given at once
to the Ruler of all! I endured much from the hateful one,
afflictions from Grendel; ever may God work
wonder upon wonder, the Shepherd of glory.
It was not long ago that I did not ever expect
to live to see a remedy for any of my miseries,
when blood-stained stood
the best of houses gory from battle,
a far-reaching misery for each of my counsellors
who despaired of ever defending
the people's fortress against foes, | [f.153v]
demons and evil spirits. Now a warrior,
through the power of the Lord, has carried out the deed
that all of us until now could not accomplish
with our skill. Indeed, she may say,
whoever was the woman who gave birth to that son
among the race of men, if she still lives,
that the God of old was gracious to her
in her child-bearing. Now, Beowulf,
best of men, as a son I will
love thee in my heart; henceforth keep well
this new kinship. Thou shalt lack no
desirable things of the world that I can command.
Full oft have I assigned reward for less,
honouring with gifts a more lowly warrior,
weaker in battle. Thou hast brought about
for thyself by thy deeds that thy glory shall live
for ever and ever. May the Ruler of all
reward thee with good, as he has done even now!'

Beowulf spoke, son of Ecgtheow:
'With much goodwill we carried out
that courageous deed, that fight, daringly risked
the strength of an unknown foe. I should have wished
rather that thou couldst have seen him,
the fiend in his trappings weary unto death!

Ic hi[ne] hrædlice   heardan clammum [f.154r]
on wælbedde   wriþan þohte,
þæt he for [mu]ndgripe   minum scolde
licgean lifbysig,   butan his lic swice.
Ic hine ne mihte,   þa Metod nolde,
ganges getwæman,   no ic him þæs georne ætfealh,
feorhgeniðlan;   wæs to foremihtig
feond on feþe.   Hwæþere he his folme forlet
to lifwraþe   last weardian,
earm ond eaxle;   no þær ænige swa þeah
feasceaft guma   frofre gebohte;
no þy leng leofað   laðgeteona
synnum geswenced,   ac hyne sar hafað
in [n]idgripe   nearwe befongen,
balwon bendum;   ðær abidan sceal
maga mane fah   miclan domes,
hu him scir Metod   scrifan wille!'
   Ða wæs swigra secg,   sunu Ec[g]lafes,
on gylpspræce   guðgeweorca,
siþðan æþelingas   eorles cræfte
ofer heanne hrof   hand sceawedon,
feondes fingras;   foran æghw[ær] wæs,
sted[e]nægla gehwylc   style gelicost,
hæþenes handsporu   hilderinces [f.154v]
egl[u] unheoru;   æghwylc gecwæð
þæt him heardra nan   hrinan wolde
iren ærgod,   þæt ðæs ahlæcan
blodge beadufolme   onberan wolde.
XV Ða wæs haten hreþe   Heort innanweard
folmum gefrætwod;   fela þæra wæs,
wera ond wifa,   þe þæt winreced.
gestsele gyredon.   Goldfag scinon
web æfter wagum,   wundorsiona fela
secga gehwylcum   þara þe on swylc starað,
Wæs þæt beorhte bold   tobrocen swiðe,
eal inneweard   irenbendum fæst,
heorras tohlidene;   hrof ana genæs
ealles ansund,   þe se aglæca
fyrendædum fag   on fleam gewand,
aldres orwena.   No þæt yðe byð
to befleonne   —fremme se þe wille—
ac ges[e]can sceal   sawlberendra
nyde genydde,   niþða bearna,
grundbuendra   gearwe stowe,
þær his lichoma   legerbedde fæst
swefeþ æfter symle.

I swiftly with | tight grips [f.154r]
thought to bind him on his death-bed,
so that because of my hand-grip he should lie
struggling for life unless his body escape.
Since the Creator did not wish it, I could not
prevent his going, I grasped him not firmly enough,
the deadly foe; the fiend was too powerful
in his going. But, he has left his hand behind,
to save his life and show his track,
his arm and shoulder; yet no comfort there
has the wretched being gained himself;
no longer lives the hateful ravager,
afflicted by sins, but pain has seized him
tightly in its inexorable grip,
with deadly bonds; there shall he await
the great Judgment, a man stained with guilt,
what the resplendent Creator will decree him!'
Then was the son of Ecglaf more silent
in vaunting speech about warlike deeds,
after the æthelings as a result of the eorl's strength
looked at the hand stretching up to the high roof,
the fingers of the foe; at the tip each one
of the firm nails was everywhere exactly like steel,
the claw of the heathen warrior, | [f.154v]
horrible, dreadful, everyone said
that no sword of proven worth
of hardy men would touch him, injure
the bloody battle-hand of that fierce assailant.
XV Then were orders swiftly given that Heorot
should be adorned within by hands; many there were,
men and women, who prepared that wine-hall,
the guest-hall. Gold-adorned gleamed
hangings on the walls, many wondrous sights
for those among men who gaze on such things.
That bright building was greatly shattered,
though fixed within by iron bands;
its door-hinges burst; the roof alone survived,
wholly unharmed, when the fierce assailant
stained with wicked deeds, turned in flight,
despairing of life. That is not easy
to flee from —let him try it who will—
but, compelled by necesity, he must seek out
the place prepared for the children of men,
for earth-dwellers possessing a soul,
where his body held fast in its grave shall sleep
after feasting.

Þa wæs sæl ond mæl
þæt to healle gang Healfdenes sunu; [f.155r]
wolde self cyning symbel þicgan.
Ne gefrægen ic þa mægþe maran weorode
ymb hyra sincgyfan sel gebæran.
Bugon þa to bence blædagande,
fylle gefægon; fægere geþægon
medoful manig magas þara
swiðhicgende on sele þam hean,
Hroðgar ond Hroþulf. Heorot innan wæs
freondum afylled; nalles facenstafas
Þeod-Scyldingas þenden fremedon.
Forgeaf þa Beowulfe brand Healfdenes
segen gyldenne sigores to leane,
hroden hil[d]ecumbor, helm ond byrnan;
mære maðþumsweord manige gesawon
beforan beorn beran. Beowulf geþah
ful on flette; no he þære feohgyfte
for sc[e]oten[d]um scamigan ðorfte.
Ne gefrægn ic freondlicor feower madmas
golde gegyrede gummanna fela
in ealobence oðrum gesellan.
Ymb þæs helmes hrof heafodbeorge
wirum bewunden wal[u] utan heold,
þæt him fela laf frecne ne meaht[e] [f.155v]
scurheard sceþðan, þonne scyldfreca
ongean gramum gangan scolde.
Heht ða eorla hleo eahta mearas
fætedhleore on flet teon,
in under eoderas; þara anum stod
sadol searwum fah, since gewurþad;
þæt wæs hildesetl heahcyninges,
ðonne sweorda gelac sunu Healfdenes
efnan wolde; næfre on ore læg
widcuþes wig, ðonne walu feollon.
Ond ða Beowulfe bega gehwæþres
eodor Ingwina onweald geteah,
wicga ond wæpna; het hine wel brucan.
Swa manlice mære þeoden,
hordweard hæleþa heaþoræsas geald
mearum ond madmum, swa hy næfre man lyhð,
se þe secgan wile soð æfter rihte.
XVI Ða gyt æghwylcum eorla drihten
þara þe mid Beowulfe briml[a]de teah,
on þære medubence maþðum gesealde,
yrfelafe, ond þone ænne heht [f.156r]

Then was it due time and fitting
that Healfdene's son should | go to the hall; [f.155r]
the king himself would partake of the feast.
Never have I heard of a people behaving better
around their treasure-giver, in a greater company.
Men of glorious renown sat down on the benches,
rejoiced in the feast; courteously drank
many a cup of mead; their kinsmen,
stout-hearted Hrothgar and Hrothulf
were in the lofty hall. Heorot within was
filled with friends; not yet then had
the Scylding people performed wicked acts.
Then Hrothgar gave Healfdene's sword to Beowulf,
a golden standard as a reward for victory,
a decorated battle-banner, helmet and byrny;
many saw the famous, precious sword
borne before the warrior. Beowulf drank
of the cup in hall; of the costly gifts
he needed not to be ashamed before the warriors.
Never have I heard of many men who
more heartily gave four gold-adorned
treasures to another on the ale-bench.
Around the helmet's crown a jutting ridge
twisted with wires guarded the head,
so that many a file-sharpened | sword, shower-hard, [f.155v]
could not sorely scathe the shield-warrior
when he had to advance against foes.
Then the protector of eorls ordered eight horses
with gold-plated bridles to be led into the hall,
within the precinct; on one of them lay
a saddle artfully decorated, adorned with jewels;
that was the war-seat of the high-king,
when the son of Healfdene wished to engage
in sword-play; never did he, renowned in war-prowess,
fail at the front when the slain fell.
And the protector of the Ingwine
conferred on Beowulf possession of both
horses and weapons; enjoined him to enjoy them well.
Thus the famous prince, the guardian
of warriors' treasure, repaid him for the battle-storms
with horses and treasures so nobly that no one who wishes
to speak the truth fairly will ever disparage them.
XVI Furthermore, the lord gave to each of the eorls,
who underoook the sea-passage with Beowulf,
treasure on the mead-bench, an | heirloom [f.156r]
and he ordered that gold be paid in recompense

golde forgyldan, þone ðe Grendel ær
mane acwealde, swa he hyra ma wolde
nefne him witig God wyrd forstode
ond ðæs mannes mod. Metod eallum weold
gumena cynnes, swa he nu git deð.
Forþan bið andgit æghwær selest,
ferhðes foreþanc; fela sceal gebidan
leofes ond laþes se þe longe her
on ðyssum windagum worolde bruceð.
Þær wæs sang ond sweg samod ætgædere
fore Healfdenes hildewisan,
gomenwudu greted, gid oft wrecen,
ðonne healgamen Hroþgares scop
æfter medobence mænan scolde,
[be] Finnes eaferum. Ða hie se fær begeat,
hæleð Healf-Dena, Hnæf Scyldinga
in Freswæle feallan scolde.
Ne huru Hildeburh herian þorfte
Eotena treowe; unsynnum wearð
beloren leofum æt þam [l]i[n]dplegan
bearnum ond broðrum; hie on gebyrd hruron,
gare | wunde; þæt wæs geomuru ides. [f.156v]
Nalles holinga Hoces dohtor
meotodsceaft bemearn, syþðan morgen com,
ða heo under swegle geseon meahte
morþorbealo maga. Þær he ær mæste heold
worolde wynne, wig ealle fornam
Finnes þegnas nemne feaum anum,
þæt he ne mehte on þæm meðelstede
wig Hengeste wiht gefeohtan,
ne þa wealafe wige forþringan
þeodnes ðegne; ac hig him geþingo budon,
þæt he him oðer flet eal gerymdon,
healle ond heahsetl, þæt hie healfre geweald
wið Eotena bearn agan moston,
ond æt feohgyftum Folcwaldan sunu
dogra gehwylce Dene weorþode,
Hengestes heap hringum wenede
efne swa swiðe sincgestreonum
fættan goldes, swa he Fresena cyn
on beorsele byldan wolde.
Ða hie getruwedon on twa healfa
fæste frioðuwære. Fin Hengeste
elne un[h]litme aðum | benemde, [f.157r]
þæt he þa wealafe weotena dome
arum heolde, þæt ðær ænig mon

for the one whom Grendel had lately killed
in his wickedness, as he would have done more
of them, if wise God and the man's courage
had not prevented that fate. The Creator ruled
over all mankind, as he still does.
Wherefore is understanding always best,
forethought of mind; much shall he experience
of weal and woe, who here long makes use
of the world in these days of strife.

There was song and music mingled
in the presence of Healfdene's battle-chief;
harp was plucked, lay oft recited,
when Hrothgar's scop was to relate a tale
as entertainment in the hall along the mead-bench
about the sons of Finn. When the sudden attack came upon them,
Hnæf of the Scyldings, hero of the Half-Danes,
was to fall on the Frisian field of slaughter.

No cause had Hildeburh indeed to praise
the loyalty of the Jutes; blameless, she was
deprived of her dear ones at the shield-play:
son and brother fell to their fate |
wounded by spears; a mournful woman that. [f.156v]
Not without cause did Hoc's daughter
mourn destiny's decree, when morning came
when she might see, beneath the sky,
the slaughter of kinsmen. Where he had previously
possessed the greatest worldly joy, war carried off
all Finn's thanes except a few only,
so that he was unable to pursue to the end
the battle against Hengest, the prince's thane,
in that meeting-place, or to dislodge the survivors
of the disaster by force; but they offered him terms,
that they should make entirely free for them another hall,
a chamber and high-seat; so that they might have possession
of half of it, sharing it with the sons of the Jutes,
and that the son of Folcwalda, at the giving of treasure,
every day would honour the Danes,
present Hengest's company with rings,
with just as much treasure
of plated gold as would greatly cheer
the Frisian race in the beer-hall.

Then they confirmed on two sides
the firm peace-treaty. To Hengest, Finn
with ill-fated courage | declared with oaths [f.157r]
that in the judgment of his counsellors he would treat
the survivors honourably, that no man there

wordum ne worcum   wære ne bræce,
ne þurh inwitsearo   æfre gemænden,
ðeah hie hira beaggyfan   banan folgedon
ðeodenlease,   þa him swa geþearfod wæs;
gyf þonne Frysna hwylc   frecn[a]n spræce
ðæs morþorhetes   myndgiend wære,
þonne hit sweordes ecg   s[e]ðan scolde.
  Að wæs geæfned,   ond i[n]cgegold
ahæfen of horde.   Here-Scyldinga
betst beadorinca   wæs on bæl gearu;
æt þæm ade wæs   eþgesyne
swatfah syrce,   swyn ealgylden,
eofer irenheard,   æþeling manig
wundum awyrded   —sume on wæle crungon.
Het ða Hildeburh   æt Hnæfes ade
hire selfre sunu   sweoloðe befæstan,
banfatu bærnan,   ond on bæl don
e[a]me on eaxle.   Ides gnornode,
geomrode giddum;   guðrinc astah;
wand | to wolcnum   wælfyra mæst,   [f.157v]
hlynode for hlawe.   Hafelan multon,
bengeato burston   ðonne blod ætspranc,
laðbite lices.   Lig ealle forswealg,
gæsta gifrost,   þara ðe þær guð fornam
bega folces;   wæs hira blæd scacen.
XVII Gewiton him ða wigend   wica neosian
freondum befeallen,   Frysland geseon,
hamas ond heaburh.   Hengest ða gyt
wælfagne winter   wunode mid Finne
[e]l[ne] unhlitme;   eard gemunde,
þeah þe he [ne] meahte   on mere drifan
hringedstefnan.   Holm storme weol,
won wið winde;   winter yþe beleac
isgebinde   oþðæt oþer com
gear in geardas,   swa nu gyt deð,
þa ðe syngales   sele bewitiað,
wuldortorhtan weder.   Ða wæs winter scacen,
fæger foldan bearm;   fundode wrecca,
gist of geardum;   he to gyrnwræce
swiðor | þohte   þonne to sælade,   [f.158r]
gif he torngemot   þurhteon mihte,
þæt he Eotena bearn   inne gemunde.
Swa he ne forwyrnde   woroldrædenne,
þonne him Hunlafing   hildeleoman,
billa selest,   on bearm dyde
—þæs wæron mid Eotenum   ecge cuðe.

should break the treaty by words or deeds,
nor through malicious design ever complain of it,
although they had served their ring-giver's slayer,
being lordless, since it was imposed on them by necessity;
if, by audacious speech, any Frisian should
recall to mind that deadly feud,
then must sword's edge settle it.
The oath was performed, and immense gold
brought from the hoard. The best of warriors
of the warlike Scyldings was ready on the pyre;
on that funeral pyre were plain to see
blood-stained mail-shirt, swine-image all-golden,
the boar hard as iron, many an ætheling
slain with wounds —some fallen in the fight.
Then Hildeburh bade her own son be given
over to the flames at Hnæf's funeral pyre,
his body burned, and placed on the pyre
at his uncle's shoulder. The woman mourned,
lamented in dirges; the warrior was raised aloft;
the greatest of funeral-fires | curled to the clouds, [f.157v]
roared before the burial-mound. Heads melted,
wound-gashes burst, as blood gushed out,
body's grievous wounds. Fire swallowed up,
greediest of spirits, those whom war carried off
of both peoples; their glory had passed away.
XVII The warriors departed to their dwellings,
deprived of friends, went to see Friesland's
homes and high stronghold. Hengest still
remained with Finn for a slaughter-stained winter,
with ill-fated courage; he remembered his homeland,
although he could not sail on the sea
his ring-prowed ship. The sea surged with storms,
contended with the wind; winter locked the waves
in icy bonds until another year came
to the dwellings of men, as it still does now,
times of gloriously bright weather that always
observe their proper seasons. Then was winter past,
earth's bosom fair; the exile eager to go,
the stranger from the dwellings; revenge for injury he | [f.158r]
thought of more than on that sea-journey,
if he might bring about a hostile encounter
so that he might remember in his heart the sons of the Jutes.
So he did not refuse the law of the world
when Hunlaf's son placed on his lap
a gleaming weapon, the finest of swords
—its edges were famous among the Jutes.

Swylce ferhðfrecan Fin eft begeat
sweordbealo sliðen æt his selfes ham,
siþðan grimne gripe Guðlaf ond Oslaf
æfter sæsiðe sorge mændon,
ætwiton weana dæl; ne meahte wæfre mod
forhabban in hreþre. Đa wæs heal [r]oden
feonda feorum, swilce Fin slægen,
cyning on corþre, ond seo cwen numen.
Sceotend Scyldinga to scypon feredon
eal ingesteald eorðcyninges,
swylce hie æt Finnes ham findan meahton
sigla searogimma. Hie on sælade
drihtlice wif to Denum feredon,
læddon | to leodum.
Leoð wæs asungen, [f.158v]
gleomannes gyd. Gamen eft astah,
beorhtode bencsweg, byrelas sealdon
win of wunderfatum. Þa cwom Wealhþeo forð
gan under gyldnum beage þær þa godan twegen
sæton suhtergefæderan; þa gyt wæs hiera sib ætgædere,
æghwylc oðrum trywe. Swylce þær [U]nferþ þyle
æt fotum sæt frean Scyldinga; gehwylc hiora his ferhþe treowde,
þæt he hæfde mod micel, þeah þe he his magum nære
arfæst æt ecga gelacum. Spræc ða ides Scyldinga:
'Onfoh þissum fulle, freodrihten min,
sinces brytta! Þu on sælum wes,
goldwine gumena, ond to Geatum spræc
mildum wordum, swa sceal man don.
Beo wið Geatas glæd, geofena gemyndig
nean ond feorran [þe] þu nu hafast.
Me man sægde þæt þu ðe for sunu wolde [f.159r]
hereri[n]c habban. Heorot is gefælsod,
beahsele beorhta; bruc þenden þu mote
manigra medo, ond þinum magum læf
folc ond rice þonne ðu forð scyle
metodsceaft seon. Ic minne can
glædne Hroþulf, þæt he þa geogoðe wile
arum healdan gyf þu ær þonne he,
wine Scildinga, worold oflætest;
wene ic þæt he mid gode gyldan wille
uncran eaferan, gif he þæt eal gemon,
hwæt wit to willan ond to worðmyndum
umborwesendum ær arna gefremedon.'
Hwearf þa bi bence þær hyre byre wæron,
Hreðric ond Hroðmund, ond hæleþa bearn,
giogoð ætgædere; þær se goda sæt,

Likewise cruel death by the sword befell
bold-hearted Finn in his own home,
when Guthlaf and Oslaf, after their sea-voyage,
spoke of the fierce attack and of their sorrow,
blamed him for their share of woes; their restless spirit
could not be restrained in their breast. Then was hall made red
with lives of foes, Finn slain also,
the king amid his troop, and the queen taken.
The Scylding warriors carried to the ship
all the house-treasure of the king of the land,
whatever they could find at Finn's home
of jewels, finely-wrought gems. On the sea-journey
they carried the lady back to the Danes,
led her | to her people.
The song was sung, [f.158v]
the gleeman's tale. Then revelry arose,
bench-noise rang out, cup-bearers dispensed
wine from wondrous vessels. Then Wealhtheow came forth,
wearing a golden circlet, to where the two valiant ones
were sitting, uncle and nephew; they were then still at peace together,
each to the other true. There, too, sat Unferth the spokesman
at the feet of the lord of the Scyldings; each of them trusted his spirit,
that he had much courage, though he was not merciful to his kinsmen
at the sword-play. Then spoke the lady of the Scyldings:
'Take this cup, my noble lord,
bestower of treasure! Be glad,
gold-giving friend of men, and speak to the Geats
with kindly words, as one ought to do.
Be gracious to the Geats, mindful of gifts
which thou now hast from near and from afar.
I have been told that | thou wouldst have the warrior [f.159r]
for a son. Heorot is cleansed,
the gleaming ring-hall; use while thou mayst
many rewards, and to thy kinsmen leave
people and kingdom when thou must pass on
to meet thy appointed fate. I know
my gracious Hrothulf, that he will treat the youths
honourably if thou, friend of the Scyldings,
sooner than he, leavest the world;
I believe that he will liberally repay
our sons, if he remembers all the favours
that we formerly did for him for his pleasure
and his honour while he was a child.'
She turned then to the bench where her sons were,
Hrethric and Hrothmund, and the sons of warriors,
young men together; where sat the valiant one,

Beowulf Geata be þæm gebroðrum twæm.
XVIII Him wæs ful boren, ond freondlaþu
wordum bewægned, ond wunden gold
estum geeawed, earm[h]reade twa,
hrægl ond hringas, healsbeaga mæst [f.159v]
þara þe ic on foldan gefrægn hæbbe.
Nænigne ic under swegle selran hyrde
hordma[ðð]um hæleþa, syþðan Hama ætwæg
to [þæ]re byrhtan byrig Brosinga mene,
sigle ond sincfæt —searoniðas f[lea]h
Eormenrices, geceas ecne ræd.
Þone hring hæfde Higelac Geata,
nefa Swertinges nyhstan siðe,
siðþan he under segne sinc ealgode,
wælreaf werede; hyne wyrd fornam,
syðþan he for wlenco wean ahsode,
fæhðe to Frysum. He þa frætwe wæg,
eorclanstanas ofer yða ful,
rice þeoden; he under rande gecranc.
Gehwearf þa in Francna fæþm feorh cyninges,
breostgewædu, ond se beah somod;
wyrsan wigfrecan wæl reafed[o]n
æfter guðsceare; Geata leode
hreawic heoldon. Heal swege onfeng.
Wealhðeo maþelode, heo fore þæm werede spræc:
'Bruc ðisses beages, Beowulf leofa,
hyse, mid hæle, ond þisses hrægles neot, [f.160r]
þeo[d]gestreona, ond geþeoh tela,
cen þec mid cræfte, ond þyssum cnyhtum wes
lara liðe. Ic þe þæs lean geman.
Hafast þu gefered, þæt ðe feor ond neah
ealne wideferhþ weras ehtigað,
efne swa side swa sæ bebugeð,
windgeard, weallas. Wes þenden þu lifige,
æþeling, eadig. Ic þe an tela
sincgestreona. Beo þu suna minum
dædum gedefe, dreamhealdende.
Her is æghwylc eorl oþrum getrywe,
modes milde, mandrihtne hol[d];
þegnas syndon geþwære, þeod ealgearo,
druncne dryhtguman doð swa ic bidde.'
Eode þa to setle. Þær wæs symbla cyst,
druncon win weras. Wyrd ne cuþon,
geosceaft grim[m]e, swa hit agangen wearð
eorla manegum, syþðan æfen cwom,
ond him Hroþgar gewat to hofe sinum,

Beowulf of the Geats, beside the two brothers.
XVIII To him was the cup carried, and cordial invitation
offered in words, and twisted gold
graciously presented: two arm-ornaments,
a garment and ring | s, the finest of neck-rings [f.159v]
of those which I have heard about on earth.
Never under heaven have I heard of a better
treasure-hoard of heroes, since Hama carried off
to the splendid stronghold the necklace of the Brosings,
the jewel and costly setting —fled the cunning enmity
of Eormenric, chose eternal gain.
That ring did Hygelac of the Geats,
the grandson of Swerting, have on his last venture,
when, beneath his banner, he defended the treasure,
protected the spoils of slaughter; Fate carried him off,
when for pride he sought trouble,
feud with the Frisians. Over the cup of the waves,
he, mighty prince, had carried the treasure,
the precious stones; he perished beneath his shield.
Then the king's body passed into the power of the Franks,
mail-coat and circlet also;
less worthy warriors plundered the slain
after the carnage of battle; the people of the Geats
held that place of corpses. The hall was filled with sound.
Wealhtheow spoke, she said before the company:
'Enjoy this circlet, beloved Beowulf,
young man, with luck, | and use this garment, [f.160r]
from the people's treasure, and prosper well,
make thyself known for valour, and to these boys
be kind in counsel. I shall remember to reward thee for that.
Thou hast brought it about that far and near
men will praise thee for ever,
just as widely as the sea encompasses
the home of the winds, the cliffs. While thou livest,
prince, be prosperous. I wish thee well
of thy rich treasure. Be kind to my son
in deeds, thou joyful one.
Here every eorl is true to the other,
mild of heart, loyal to his lord;
the thanes are united, the people fully prepared,
retainers cheered with drink do as I ask.'
Then she went to her seat. There was the best of feasts,
men drank wine. They knew not fate,
dread destiny, as it came to pass
for many eorls, after evening came,
and Hrothgar went to his dwelling,

rice to ræste. Reced weardode
unrim eorla, swa hie oft ær dydon.
Bencþelu beredon; hit geondbræded wearð
beddum ond bolstrum. Beorscealca sum
fus ond fæge fletræste gebeag. [f.160v]
Setton him to heafdon hilderandas,
bordwudu beorhtan; þær on bence wæs
ofer æþelinge yþgesene
heaþosteapa helm, hringed byrne,
þrecwudu þrymlic. Wæs þeaw hyra,
þæt hie oft wæron an wig gearwe,
ge æt ham ge on herge, ge gehwæþer þara
efne swylce mæla, swylce hira mandryhtne
þearf gesealde; wæs seo þeod tilu.
XVIIII Sigon þa to slæpe. Sum sare angeald
æfenræste, swa him ful oft gelamp
siþðan goldsele Grendel warode,
unriht æfnde oþþæt ende becwom,
swylt æfter synnum. Þæt gesyne wearþ,
widcuþ werum, þætte wrecend þa gyt
lifde æfter laþum lange þrage,
æfter guðceare. Grendles modor,
ides aglæcwif yrmþe gemunde,
se þe wæteregesan wunian scolde,
cealde streamas, siþðan Ca[in] wearð
to ecgbanan angan breþer,
fæderenmæge; he þa fag gewat,
morþre gemearcod, | mandream fleon, [f.161r]
westen warode. Þanon woc fela
geocsceaftgasta; wæs þæra Grendel sum,
heorowearh hetelic, se æt Heorote fand
wæccendne wer wiges bidan.
Þær him aglæca ætgræpe wearð;
hwæþre he gemunde mægenes strenge,
gimfæste gife ðe him God sealde,
ond him to Anwaldan are gelyfde,
frofre ond fultum; ðy he þone feond ofercwom,
gehnægde helle gast. Þa he hean gewat,
dreame bedæled deaþwic seon,
mancynnes feond; ond his modor þa gyt
gifre ond galgmod gegan wolde
sorhfulne sið, sunu [d]eo[ð] wrecan.
Com þa to Heorote, ðær Hring-Dene
geond þæt sæld swæfun. Þa ðær sona wearð
edhwyrft eorlum, siþðan inne fealh
Grendles modor. Wæs se gryre læssa

the chieftain to his place of rest. A countless number of eorls
guarded the hall, as they had often done before.
They cleared the bench-boards; it was spread over
with beds and bolsters. One of the feasters,
ready and fated to die, | lay down on his hall-couch. [f.160v]
They set at their heads their battle-shields,
bright bucklers; there on the bench,
above each ætheling were easily visible
helmet that towered in battle, ringed byrny,
mighty spear. It was their custom
to be constantly ready for war,
both at home and in the field, and in either case
at whatever times need came upon
their liege lord; that was a good people.
XVIIII Then they sank to sleep. One man paid sorely
for his night's rest, as had oft befallen them
after Grendel occupied the gold-hall,
carried out wrong, until the end came,
death after sins. It became manifest,
widely known to men, that an avenger still
lived after the hostile foe a long time,
after the grievous strife. Grendel's mother,
a she-monster, had in mind her misery,
she who had to inhabit fearsome water,
cold streams, after Cain became
the sword-slayer of his only brother,
a kinsman on his father's side; he went outlawed,
to flee | human joy, marked with murder, [f.161r]
dwelt in the wilderness. From him sprang many
spirits sent by fate, of whom Grendel was one,
a hateful savage outcast, who at Heorot found
a watching man, waiting for battle.
There the fierce assailant took hold of him;
yet he bore in mind the mighty strength,
the ample gift that God gave him,
and relied on favour from the Ruler,
solace and support; because of that he overcame the foe,
laid low the hell-spirit. Then he went, humiliated,
deprived of joy, to seek his death-place,
mankind's enemy; and his mother, still
greedy and gloomy, wished to enter upon
a sorrowful journey, avenge her son's death.
She came then to Heorot, where the Ring-Danes
were sleeping throughout the hall. Then soon came
a change for the eorls there, when Grendel's mother
entered in. The attack was less terrible

efne swa micle swa bið mægþa cræft,
wiggryre wifes be wæpnedmen,
þonne heoru bunden, hamere geþ[ru]en,
sweord swate fah swin ofer helme
ecgum | dyh[t]ig andweard scireð. [f.161v]
Þa wæs on healle heardecg togen
sweord ofer setlum, sidrand manig
hafen handa fæst; helm ne gemunde,
byrnan side, þa hine se broga angeat.
Heo wæs on ofste, wolde ut þanon,
feore beorgan þa heo onfunden wæs;
hraðe heo æþelinga anne hæfde
fæste befangen þa heo to fenne gang.
Se wæs Hroþgare hæleþa leofost
on gesiðes had be sæm tweonum,
rice randwiga, þone ðe heo on ræste abreat,
blædfæstne beorn. Næs Beowulf ðær,
ac wæs oþer in ær geteohhod
æfter maþðumgife mærum Geate.
Hream wearð in Heorote; heo under heolfre genam
cuþe folme; cearu wæs geniwod,
geworden in wicun. Ne wæs þæt gewrixle til,
þæt hie on ba healfa bicgan scoldon
freonda feorum.
                Þa wæs frod cyning,
har hilderinc, on hreon | mode, [f.162r]
syðþan he aldorþegn unlyfigendne,
þone deorestan deadne wisse.
Hraþe wæs to bure Beowulf fetod,
sigoreadig secg. Samod ærdæge
eode eorla sum, æþele cempa
self mid gesiðum þær se snotera bad,
hwæþ[er] him A[l]walda æfre wille
æfter weaspelle wyrpe gefremman.
Gang ða æfter flore fyrdwyrðe man
mid his handscale —healwudu dynede—
þæt he þone wisan wordum [n]ægde
frean Ingwina, frægn gif him wære
æfter neodlaðu[m] niht getæse.
XX Hroðgar maþelode, helm Scyldinga:
'Ne frin þu æfter sælum! Sorh is geniwod
Denigea leodum. Dead is Æschere,
Yrmenlafes yldra broþor,
min runwita ond min rædbora,
eaxlgestealla, ðonne we on orlege
hafelan weredon, þonne hniton feþan,

by just so much as is women's strength,
a woman's war-terror, than an armed man's,
when the ornamented, hammer-forged blade,
the blood-stained sword, | strong of edge, [f.161v]
shears the boar-image on an enemy's helm.
Then in the hall was hard-edged sword
drawn over seats, many a broad shield
raised in firm hand; no one thought of the helm,
of the broad byrny, when terror seized him.
She was in haste, wished to depart thence,
save her life when she was discovered;
swiftly she seized one of the æthelings
firmly when she fled to the fen.
To Hrothgar he was the dearest of heroes
between the seas of the rank of retainer,
a mighty shield-warrior, a man of great repute,
whom she killed in his place of rest. Beowulf was not there,
for earlier, another lodging-place had been assigned
the famous Geat, after the treasure-giving.
There was uproar in Heorot; she had carried off
the well-known hand in its gore; sorrow was renewed,
came about in the dwelling-place. That was no good exchange,
that they had to pay for on both sides
with lives of friends.
Then was the old king,
the grizzled warrior, troubled in heart, | [f.162r]
when he knew that his chief thane was lifeless,
the dearest one dead.
Quickly was Beowulf fetched to the chamber,
the victory-blest man. At daybreak together
with other eorls he went, the noble warrior
himself with his companions, to where the wise one waited,
to see whether the Ruler of all would ever
bring about a change, after the tidings of woe.
Then the man distinguished in war walked across the floor
with his troop of retainers —hall-timbers resounded—
until he addressed with words the wise lord
of the Ingwine, asked if he had had an agreeable night
after his invitation to convivial pleasure.
XX Hrothgar spoke, protector of the Scyldings:
'Ask not thou after joy! Sorrow is renewed
for the people of the Danes. Æschere is dead,
Yrmenlaf's elder brother,
my confidant and counsellor, my adviser,
my close comrade, when in battle we
defended our heads, when foot-troops clashed,

eoferas cynsedan. Swy[lc] scolde eorl wesan, [f.162v]
[æþeling] ærgod, swylc Æschere wæs!
Wearð him on Heorote to handbanan
wælgæst wæfre; ic ne wat hwæþer
atol æse wlanc eftsiðas teah,
fylle gef[æ]gnod. Heo þa fæhðe wræc,
þe þu gystran niht Grendel cwealdest
þurh hæstne had heardum clammum,
forþan he to lange leode mine
wanode ond wyrde. He æt wige gecrang
ealdres scyldig, ond nu oþer cwom
mihtig manscaða, wolde hyre mæg wrecan,
ge feor hafað fæhðe gestæled,
þæs þe þincean mæg þegne monegum
se þe æfter sincgyfan on sefan greoteþ,
hreþerbealo hearde; nu seo hand ligeð
se þe eow welhwylcra wilna dohte.
Ic þæt londbuend, leode mine,
selerædende secgan hyrde,
þæt hie gesawon swylce twegen
micle mearcsteapan moras healdan,
ellorgæstas. Ðæra oðer wæs,
þæs þe hie gewislicost gewitan meahton,
idese onlicn[e]s; oðer earmsceapen
on weres wæstmum wræclastas | træd, [f.163r]
næfne he wæs mara þonne ænig man oðer;
þone on geardagum Grendel nemdo[n]
foldbuende; no hie fæder cunnon,
hwæþer him ænig wæs ær acenned
dyrnra gasta. Hie dygel lond
warigeað, wulfhleoþu, windige næssas,
frecne fengelad, ðær fyrgenstream
under næssa genipu niþer gewiteð,
flod under foldan. Nis þæt feor heonon
milgemearces, þæt se mere stan[d]eð;
ofer þæm hongiað hrinde bearwas,
wudu wyrtum fæst wæter oferhelmað.
Þær mæg nihta gehwæm niðwundor seon,
fyr on flode. No þæs frod leofað
gumena bearna þæt þone grund wite.
Ðeah þe hæðstapa hundum geswenced,
heorot hornum trum holtwudu sece,
feorran geflymed, ær he feorh seleð,
aldor on ofre, ær he in wille,
hafelan [hydan]. Nis þæt heoru stow!
Þonon yðgeblond up astigeð

hewed helms. | Such should an eorl be, [f.162v]
[an ætheling] of proven excellence, as was Æschere.
In Heorot now a wandering deadly creature
has slain him with her hands; I know not whether
the terrible creature journeyed back, glorying in carrion,
made glad by that feast. She has avenged the hostile deed,
in which yester-night thou didst violently kill
Grendel with hard grips,
because he too long had reduced and injured
my people. He fell in battle,
having forfeited life, and now comes another
mighty wicked ravager, would avenge her kinsman,
and has gone far in taking vengeance for that feud,
as it may seem to many a thane
who mourns his treasure-giver in his heart,
a heavy sorrow; now lifeless lies the hand
which helped your every desire.
  Country-dwellers, folk of mine,
hall-counsellors, I have heard,
say that they saw two such
huge prowlers of the marshes hold the moors,
alien beings. One of these was,
as far as they could most certainly discover,
of a woman's likeness; the other wretched creature
in man's form | trod exile-tracks, [f.163r]
except he was mightier than any other man;
whom dwellers in the land in former times
called Grendel; they know of no father,
whether there had been born to him earlier any such
mysterious being. A secret land
they haunt, wolf-ridden slopes, windy headlands,
perilous fen-paths, where the mountain stream
descends under misty cliffs,
a flood under the earth. It is not far hence,
measured in miles, that the mere stands;
over it hang rime-girt groves,
the firm-rooted wood overshadows the water.
There each night a fearful wonder may be seen,
fire on the flood. There is no one alive among
the children of men so wise as to know the bottom.
Though harassed by hounds, the heath-stalker,
the stag strong in antlers, driven from afar,
would rather seek the holt, give up his life,
his spirit, on the bank, than [hide] his head
in there. That is no pleasant place!
From there the surging waves rise up,

won to wolcnum, þonne wind styreþ
lað gewidru, oðþæt lyft drysmaþ,
roderas reotað. Nu is se ræd gelang
eft æt þe anum. Eard git ne const, [f.163v]
frecne stowe, ðær þu findan miht
sinnigne secg; sec gif þu dyrre!
Ic þe þa fæhðe feo leanige,
ealdgestreonum, swa ic ær dyde,
wund[num] golde, gyf þu on weg cymest.'

XXI Beowulf maþelode, bearn Ecgþeowes:
'Ne sorga, snotor guma! Selre bið æghwæm
þæt he his freond wrece þonne he fela murne.
Ure æghwylc sceal ende gebidan
worolde lifes; wyrce se þe mote
domes ær deaþe; þæt bið drihtguman
unlifgendum æfter selest.
Aris, rices weard, uton hraþe feran,
Grendles magan gang sceawigan.
Ic hit þe gehate: no he on helm losaþ,
ne on foldan fæþm, ne on fyrgenholt
ne on gyfenes grund, ga þær he wille!
Ðys dogor þu geþyld hafa
weana gehwylces, swa ic þe wene to.'
Ahleop ða se gomela, Gode þancode,
mihtigan Drihtne, þæs se man gespræc. [f.164r]

Þa wæs Hroðgare hors gebæted,
wicg wundenfeax. Wisa fengel
geatolic gende; gumfeþa stop
lindhæbbendra. Lastas wæron
æfter waldswaþum wide gesyne,
gang ofer grundas, [swa] gegnum for
ofer myrcan mor, magoþegna bær
þone selestan sawolleasne
þara þe mid Hroðgare ham eahtode.
Ofereode þa æþelinga bearn
steap stanhliðo, stige nearwe,
enge anpaðas, uncuð gelad,
neowle næssas, nicorhusa fela
He feara sum beforan gengde
wisra monna wong sceawian,
oþþæt he færinga fyrgenbeamas
ofer harne stan hleonian funde,
wynleasne wudu; wæter under stod
dreorig ond gedrefed. Denum eallum wæs,
winum Scyldinga weorce on mode
to geþolianne, ðegne monegum,

dark to the clouds, when the wind stirs up
grievous storms, until the air becomes gloomy,
the skies weep. Now is help dependent
again on | thee alone. Thou dost not yet know the region, [f.163v]
the perilous place, where thou mayst find
the sinful creature; seek it if thou darest!
I will reward thee for the feud with wealth,
with ancient treasure, as I did before,
with twisted gold, if thou comest away alive.'

XXI Beowulf spoke, son of Ecgtheow:
'Sorrow not, wise warrior! Better is it for each
that he avenge his friend than greatly mourn.
Each of us must experience the end
of life in the world; let him who may
achieve glory before death; that is best
for a warrior when life is over.
Arise, guardian of the kingdom; let us go quickly,
to look at the trail of Grendel's kinswoman.
I promise thee: she shall not escape to protection,
nor in earth's bosom, nor in mountain wood,
nor at the bottom of the sea, go where she will.
This day do thou have patience
in every misery, as I expect thee to.'
Then the old man leapt up, thanked God,
the mighty Lord, for what the man | spoke. [f.164r]

Then was Hrothgar's horse bridled,
a steed with braided mane. The wise king
rode in fine array: the foot-troop marched,
bearing shields. Footprints were
visible widely along the forest paths,
tracks over the ground, [as] she went straight
over the murky moor, bore
the best of thanes, lifeless,
who watched over their home with Hrothgar.
The son of æthelings strode across
the steep rocky slopes, narrow paths,
straitened tracks —an unknown way,
beetling crags, many a water-monster's home.
He went on ahead with a few wise men
to examine the place,
until suddenly he found the mountain trees
leaning out over grey rock,
a joyless wood; the water below lay
blood-stained and turbid. For all the Danes,
the friends of the Scyldings, it was painful at heart
to suffer, for many a thane,

oncyð eorla gehwæm, syðþan Æscheres
on þam holmclife hafelan metton.
Flod blode weol —folc to sægon—
hatan heolfre. Horn stundum song [f.164v]
fuslic f[yrd]leoð. Feþa eal gesæt.
Gesawon ða æfter wætere wyrmcynnes fela,
sellice sædracan sund cunnian,
swylce on næshleoðum nicras licgean,
ða on undernmæl oft bewitigað
sorhfulne sið on seglrade,
wyrmas ond wildeor. Hie on weg hruron
bitere ond gebolgne; bearhtm ongeaton,
guðhorn galan. Sumne Geata leod
of flanbogan feores getwæfde,
yðgewinnes, þæt him on aldre stod
herestræl hearda; he on holme wæs
sundes þe sænra, ðe hyne swylt fornam.
Hræþe wearð on yðum mid eoferspreotum
heorohocyhtum hearde genearwod,
niða genæged, ond on næs togen,
wundorlic wægbora; weras sceawedon
gryrelicne gist.
Gyrede hine Beowulf
eorlgewædum, nalles for ealdre mearn;
scolde herebyrne hondum gebroden,
sid ond searofah sund cunnian,
seo ðe bancofan beorgan cuþe,
þæt him hildegrap hreþre ne mihte,
eorres inwitfeng aldre gesceþðan;
ac se hwita helm hafelan werede, [f.165r]
se þe meregrundas mengan scolde,
secan sundgebland since geweorðad,
befongen freawrasnum, swa hine fyrndagum
worhte wæpna smið, wundrum teode,
besette swinlicum, þæt hine syðþan no
brond ne beadomecas bitan ne meahton.
Næs þæt þonne mætost mægenfultuma,
þæt him on ðearle lah ðyle Hroðgares:
wæs þæm hæftmece Hrunting nama;
þæt wæs an foran ealdgestreona;
ecg wæs iren, atertanum fah,
ahyrded heaþoswate; næfre hit æt hilde ne swac
manna ængum þara þe hit mid mundum bewand,
se ðe gryresiðas gegan dorste,
folcstede fara; næs þæt forma sið
þæt hit ellenweorc æfnan scolde.

grief to each of the eorls, when they found
Æschere's head on the cliff by the water-side.
The flood seethed with blood, with | hot gore: [f.164v]
the people gazed on it. At times the horn sang
an urgent war-song. The foot-troop all sat down.
Then they saw within the water many of the serpent race,
strange sea-dragons exploring the water,
on the cliff-slopes, too, they saw water-monsters lie,
who in the morning-time oft undertake
a sorrow-bringing journey on the sail-road,
serpents and wild beasts. These rushed away,
fierce and enraged; they had heard the sound,
the war-horn resound. A man of the Geats
with an arrow from his bow, severed one from life,
from its struggle against the waves, so that the hard
war-arrow stuck in its vitals; it was the slower
at swimming in the water, as death carried it off.
Quickly it was hard pressed in the waves
with savagely-barbed boar-spears,
fiercely attacked, and dragged on the headland,
a wondrous wave-roamer; men examined
the dread stranger.
Beowulf dressed himself
in warrior's garb; he felt no fear for his life;
his war-corselet, hand-woven,
broad and well-wrought, was to explore the water;
it was able to to protect his body,
so that the hostile grasp might not harm his breast,
the furious foe's malicious clutch, his life;
but the gleaming helmet guarded his | head, [f.165r]
which was to stir up the bottom of the mere,
enter the surging water, embellished with gold,
encircled with lordly bands, as in days of old
the weapon smith had made it, wondrously formed it,
set it round with boar-images, so that after that no
sword or battle-blade might ever bite into it.
That was not the least of powerful helps
which Hrothgar's spokesman lent him in his need:
Hrunting was the name of the hilted sword;
it was one of the foremost of ancient treasures;
the blade was of iron, gleaming with twigs of venom,
hardened in the blood of battle; never in war had it failed
any man, of those who grasped it with their hands,
who dared enter upon perilous expeditions,
the meeting-place of foes; that was not the first time
that it had to perform a courageous deed.

Huru ne gemunde   mago Ecglafes,
eafoþes cræftig,   þæt he ær gespræc
wine druncen,   þa he þæs wæpnes onlah
selran sweordfrecan.   Selfa ne dorste
under yða gewin   aldre geneþan,
drihtscype dreogan;   þær he dome forleas,
ellenmærðum.   Ne wæs þæm oðrum swa, [f.165v]
syðþan he hine to guðe   gegyred hæfde.
XXII Beowulf maþelode,   bearn Ecgþeowes:
'Geþenc nu, se mæra   maga Healfdenes,
snottra fengel,   nu ic eom siðes fus,
goldwine gumena,   hwæt wit geo spræcon,
gif ic æt þearfe   þinre scolde
aldre linnan,   þæt ðu me a wære
forðgewitenum   on fæder stæle.
Wes þu mundbora   minum magoþegnum,
hondgesellum,   gif mec hild nime;
swylce þu ða madmas   þe þu me sealdest,
Hroðgar leofa,   Higelace onsend.
Mæg þonne on þæm golde ongitan   Geata dryhten,
geseon sunu Hrædles,   þonne he on þæt sinc starað,
þæt ic gumcystum   godne funde
beaga bryttan,   breac þonne moste.
Ond þu [U]nferð læt   ealde life,
wrætlic wægsweord   widcuðne man
heardecg habban;   ic me mid Hruntinge
dom gewyrce,   oþðe mec deað nimeð!' [f.166r]
Æfter þæm wordum   Weder-Geata leod
efste mid elne   —nalas andsware
bidan wolde;   brimwylm onfeng
hilderince.   Ða wæs hwil dæges
ær he þone grundwong   ongytan mehte.
Sona þæt onfunde   se ðe floda begong
heorogifre beheold   hund missera,
grim ond grædig,   þæt þær gumena sum
ælwihta eard   ufan cunnode.
Grap þa togeanes,   guðrinc gefeng
atolan clommum;   no þy ær in gescod
halan lice;   hring utan ymbbearh,
þæt heo þone fyrdhom   ðurhfon ne mihte,
locene leoðosyrcan   laþan fingrum.
Bær þa seo brimwyl[f],   þa heo to botme com,
hringa þengel   to hofe sinum,
swa he ne mihte,   no he þæ[s] modig wæs,
wæpna gewealdan,   ac hine wundra þæs fela
swe[n]cte on sunde,   sædeor monig

Indeed the son of Ecglaf, powerful in strength,
did not bear in mind what he had said before,
drunk with wine, when he lent the weapon
to a better sword-warrior. Himself he durst not
venture his life under the turmoil of the waves,
perform heroic deeds; there he lost glory,
fame for | courage. It was not so with the other, [f.165v]
when he prepared himself for battle.

XXII Beowulf spoke, son of Ecgtheow:
'Think, now, famous son of Healfdene,
wise king, now I am ready for the venture,
gold-giving friend of men, what we two spoke of formerly,
if I, in thy need, should
lose my life, that thou shouldst always be
in the place of a father when I am gone.
Be thou a protector to my young thanes,
my close comrades, if battle should take me;
and do thou also send to Hygelac the treasures
thou gavest me, dear Hrothgar.
The lord of the Geats may then perceive by that gold,
the son of Hrethel see, when he gazes on that treasure,
that I have found a good ring-giver
excellent in his bounty, had joy of him while I could.
And do thou let Unferth, widely-known man,
have the wondrous wave-patterned sword, hard of edge,
the ancient heirloom; with Hrunting I
shall achieve glory, | or death shall carry me off!' [f.166r]

After these words the man of the Weder-Geats
hastened with courage —would not at all
wait for an answer; the surging water received
the warrior. It was a brief space of time
ere he could discern the bottom.
Soon she, who had occupied the flood's expanse
a hundred half-years, fiercely ravenous,
grim and greedy, discovered that a man
was exploring from above the monsters' lair.
She grasped at him then, seized the warrior
in a terrible grip; yet she injured not
the unharmed body; ring-mail protected it around
so that she could not get through the corselet,
the linked mail-shirt, with her loathsome claws.
When she came to the bottom, the sea-wolf bore
the ring-clad prince to her dwelling,
so that he could not (no matter how brave he was)
wield weapons, for so many of the weird creatures
pressed him hard in the water, many a sea-beast

hildetuxum heresyrcan bræc,
ehton aglæcan. Đa se eorl ongeat,
þæt he [in] niðsele nathwylcum wæs,
þær him nænig wæter wihte ne sceþede,
ne him for hrofsele hrinan ne mehte
færgripe flodes; | fyrleoht geseah, [f.166v]
blacne leoman beorhte scinan.
Ongeat þa se goda grundwyrgenne,
merewif mihtig; mægenræs forgeaf
hildebille, ho[n]d swen[g]ne ofteah,
þæt hire on hafelan hringmæl agol
grædig guðleoð. Đa se gist onfand,
þæt se beadoleoma bitan nolde,
aldre sceþðan, ac seo ecg geswac
ðeodne æt þearfe; ðolode ær fela
hondgemota, helm oft gescær,
fæges fyrdhrægl; ða wæs forma sið
deorum madme þæt his dom alæg.
Eft wæs anræd, nalas elnes læt,
mærða gemyndig mæg Hylaces:
wearp ða wunde[n]mæl wrættum gebunden
yrre oretta, þæt hit on eorðan læg,
stið ond stylecg; strenge getruwode,
mundgripe mægenes. Swa sceal man don,
þonne he æt guðe gegan þenceð
longsumne lof; na ymb his lif cearað.
Gefeng þa be [f]eax[e] —nalas for fæhðe mearn—
Guð-Geata leod Grendles modor;
brægd þa beadwe heard, þa he gebolgen wæs,
feorhgeniðlan, þæt heo on flet gebeah.
Heo him eft hraþe [a]ndlean forgeald
grim | man grapum ond him togeanes feng; [f.167r]
oferwearp þa werigmod wigena strengest,
feþecempa, þæt he on fylle wearð.
Ofsæt þa þone selegyst, ond hyre sea[x] geteah
brad [ond] brunecg; wolde hire bearn wrecan,
angan eaferan. Him on eaxle læg
breostnet broden; þæt gebearh feore,
wið ord ond wið ecge ingang forstod.
Hæfde ða forsiðod sunu Ecgþeowes
under gynne grund, Geata cempa,
nemne him heaðobyrne helpe gefremede,
herenet hearde —ond halig God
geweold wigsigor; witig Drihten,
rodera Rædend hit on ryht gesced
yðelice syþðan he eft astod.

pierced his war-shirt with warlike-tusks,
fierce assailants pursued him. Then the eorl perceived
that he was in some hostile hall,
where water harmed him not at all, nor could
the sudden pull of the flood reach him
because of the roofed hall, he saw | the light of a fire, [f.166v]
a gleaming light shine brightly.

Then the valiant one saw the accursed female of the deep,
the mighty mere-wife; he gave a mighty thrust
with his battle-sword; his hand withheld not the stroke,
so that the ring-patterned sword sang about her head
a greedy war-song. Then the stranger discovered
that the battle-light would not bite,
harm life; but the blade failed
the prince in need; it had in the past endured many
a hand-to-hand battle, often sheared the helm,
the corselet of a man fated to die; that was the first time
for the rare treasure that its repute failed.

Once again the kinsman of Hygelac was resolute,
not at all slack in courage, intent on glorious deeds;
then the angry warrior threw down the patterned blade
with its inlaid ornaments, so that it lay on the ground,
hard and steel-edged; he trusted in his strength,
the might of his hand-grip. So must a man do
when he is minded in battle to gain
lasting praise: he cares not about his life.
The man of the War-Geats then seized Grendel's
mother by the hair —he grieved not at the struggle—
hardy in battle, enraged as he was,
he flung his deadly foe so that she fell on the floor.
In turn she quickly paid him back
with fierce | grasps and clutched at him; [f.167r]
then weary-hearted, the strongest of fighters,
the foot-warrior, stumbled so that he fell.
Then she sat on the hall-guest and drew her dagger,
broad and bright-edged; she was minded to avenge her son,
her only offspring. Upon his shoulder lay
the woven mail-coat; that protected his life,
prevented entry of point and edge.
The son of Ecgtheow, the warrior of the Geats,
would then have perished under the wide earth,
if his war-corselet had not provided help,
his stout mail-coat —and holy God
achieved victory in war; the wise Lord,
Ruler of the heavens, decided it aright,
easily, when he stood up again.

XXIII Geseah ða on searwum   sigeeadig bil,
ealdsweord eotenisc   ecgum þyhtig,
wigena weorðmynd;   þæt [wæs] wæpna cyst,
buton hit wæs mare   ðonne ænig mon oðer
to beadulace   ætberan meahte,
god ond geatolic,   giganta geweorc.
He gefeng þa fetelhilt,   freca Scyldinga,
hreoh ond heorogrim,   hringmæl gebrægd
aldres orwena,   yrringa sloh [f.167v]
þæt hire wið halse   heard grapode,
banhringas bræc.   Bil eal ðurhwod
fægne flæschoman;   heo on flet gecrong.
Sweord wæs swatig,   secg weorce gefeh.
   Lixte se leoma,   leoht inne stod,
efne swa of hefene   hadre scineð
rodores candel.   He æfter recede wlat;
hwearf þa be wealle,   wæpen hafenade
heard be hiltum   Higelaces ðegn,
yrre ond anræd.   Næs seo ecg fracod
hilderince,   ac he hraþe wolde
Grendle forgyldan   guðræsa fela
ðara þe he geworhte   to West-Denum
oftor micle   ðonne on ænne sið,
þonne he Hroðgares   heorðgeneatas
sloh on sweofote,   slæpende fræt
folces Denigea   fyftyne men,
ond oðer swylc   ut offerede,
laðlicu lac.   He him þæs lean forgeald,
reþe cempa,   to ðæs þe he on ræste geseah
guðwerigne   Grendel licgan
aldorleasne,   swa him ær gescod
hild æt Heorote.   Hra wide sprong
syþðan he æfter deaðe   drepe þrowade,
heorosweng heardne,   ond hine þa heafde becearf.
   Sona þæt gesawon   snottre | ceorlas, [f.168r]
þa ðe mid Hroðgare   on holm wliton,
þæt wæs yðgeblond   eal gemenged,
brim blode fah.   Blondenfeaxe,
gomele ymb godne   ongeador spræcon,
þæt hig þæs æðelinges   eft ne wendon,
þæt he sigehreðig   secean come
mærne þeoden;   þa ðæs monige gewearð
þæt hine seo brimwylf   abr[o]ten hæfde.
Ða com non dæges.   Næs ofgeafon
hwate Scyldingas;   gewat him ham þonon
goldwine gumena.   Gistas se[t]an

XXIII He saw then among the arms a victory-blest blade,
an old sword made by giants, strong in its edges,
the glory of warriors; that [was] the best of weapons,
except that it was greater than any other man
could carry to the battle-play,
good and splendid, the work of giants.
The Scylding warrior, fierce and deadly grim, seized
the belted hilt, drew the ring-patterned sword,
despairing of life, | struck angrily [f.167v]
so that the hard weapon caught her on the neck,
broke the bone-rings. The blade passed through
her fated body; on the floor she fell.
The sword was bloody, the man rejoiced in his deed.
The gleam shone, the light appeared within,
just as heaven's candle from the sky
shines brightly. He looked about the hall;
then he turned to the wall; Hygelac's thane,
angry and resolute, raised his weapon
firmly by its hilts. The blade was not useless
to the warrior, but he was minded quickly
to repay Grendel for the many attacks
he had carried out on the West-Danes,
much oftener than on one occasion,
when he slew Hrothgar's hearth-companions
in their sleep, devoured fifteen men
of the Danish people while they slumbered,
and carried off as many again,
a loathsome booty. He had paid him his reward for that,
the fierce warrior, so that he saw Grendel,
worn out by warfare, lying lifeless
in his resting-place, as the battle in Heorot
had injured him before. The body burst wide open
when it suffered a blow, a hard sword-stroke
after death; and then he hewed off his head.
Straightway the wise | ceorls [f.168r]
who gazed on the water with Hrothgar
saw that the surging waves were stirred up,
the water stained with blood. Grey-haired,
old, they spoke together about the valiant man,
that they did not expect the ætheling again
would come, victorious, to seek
the famous king; for many concluded
that the she-wolf of the water had destroyed him.
Then came the ninth hour of the day. The bold
Scyldings left the headland; thence the gold-giving
friend of men departed homewards. The strangers sat

modes seoce, ond on mere staredon;
wiston —ond ne wendon— þæt hie heora winedrihten
selfne gesawon. Þa þæt sweord ongan
æfter heaþoswate hildegicelum,
wigbil wanian. Þæt wæs wundra sum,
þæt hit eal gemealt ise gelicost,
ðonne forstes bend Fæder onlæteð,
onwindeð wælrapas, se geweald hafað
sæla ond mæla; þæt is soð Metod.
Ne nom he in þæm wicum, Weder-Geata leod,
maðmæhta ma, þeh he þær monige geseah,
buton þone hafelan ond þa hilt somod
since fage. Sweord ær gemealt,
forbarn brodenmæl; wæs þæt blod | to þæs hat, [f.168v]
ættren ellorgæst se þær inne swealt.
Sona wæs on sunde se þe ær æt sæcce gebad
wighryre wraðra, wæter up þurhdeaf;
wæron yðgebland eal gefælsod,
eacne eardas, þa se ellorgast
oflet lifdagas ond þas lænan gesceaft.
Com þa to lande lidmanna helm
swiðmod swymman; sælace gefeah,
mægenbyrþenne þara þe he him mid hæfde.
Eodon him þa togeanes, Gode þancodon,
ðryðlic þegna heap, þeodnes gefegon,
þæs þe hi hyne gesundne geseon moston.
Ða wæs of þæm hroran helm ond byrne
lungre alysed. Lagu drusade,
wæter under wolcnum, wældreore fag.
Ferdon forð þonon feþelastum
ferhþum fægne, foldweg mæton,
cuþe stræte. Cyningbalde men
from þæm holmclife hafelan bæron
earfoðlice heora æghwæþrum
felamodigra; feower scoldon
on þæm wælstenge weorcum geferian
to þæm goldsele Grendles heafod,
oþðæt | semninga to sele comon [f.169r]
frome fyrdhwate feowertyne
Geata gongan. Gumdryhten mid
modig on gemonge meodowongas træd.
Ða com in gan ealdor ðegna,
dædcene mon dome gewurþad,
hæle hildedeor, Hroðgar gretan.
Þa wæs be feaxe on flet boren
Grendles heafod, þær guman druncon,

sick at heart, and stared at the mere;
they wished —but did not expect— they would
see their friendly lord himself. Then, because of the blood
shed in combat, the sword, that war-blade, began
to waste away into icicles of battle. That was a wondrous thing
that it all melted away, most like ice
when the Father loosens the bonds of frost,
unwinds the flood-ropes; He has power
over seasons and times; that is the true Creator.
The man of the Weder-Geats took not from the dwelling-place
more precious possessions, although he saw many there,
except the head, and also the hilts,
adorned with treasure. The sword had melted away before,
the patterned blade burned up; the blood had been | so hot, [f.168v]
the alien being so poisonous, who died therein.
Soon he was swimming who had lived through the fall
of foes in battle; he dived up through the water;
the vast tracts of surging waves
were all cleansed, when the alien being
left the days of his life and this transitory world.
Then came the protector of seamen to land,
swimming boldly; rejoiced in his sea-booty,
the mighty burden of those which he had with him.
Then the mighty band of thanes, went towards him,
thanked God, rejoiced over their prince,
that they were able to see him unharmed.
Then helm and byrny from the sturdy one
were quickly loosened. The lake grew calm,
water beneath the clouds, stained with the blood of battle.
They went forth thence on foot-tracks,
glad at heart, traversed the path,
the well-known road. Men brave as a king
bore the head from the sea-girt cliff
with difficulty for each of those
very brave ones; four were needed
to carry Grendel's head with difficulty
on a pole for the slain to the gold-hall,
until | presently the fourteen bold Geats, [f.169r]
valiant in war, came striding to the hall. Among them,
proud in the throng, the lord of men
walked on the ground by the mead-hall.
Then in came the leader of the thanes,
valiant in deeds, exalted by renown,
the warrior brave in battle, to greet Hrothgar.
Then was Grendel's head borne by the hair
over the hall-floor, where men were drinking,

egeslic for eorlum   ond þære idese mid,
wliteseon wrætlic;   weras on sawon.
XXIIII Beowulf maþelode,   bearn Ecgþeowes:
'Hwæt, we þe þas sælac,   sunu Healfdenes,
leod Scyldinga,   lustum brohton
tires to tacne,   þe þu her to locast.
Ic þæt unsofte   ealdre gedigde
wigge under wætere,   weorc geneþde
earfoðlice;   ætrihte wæs
guð getwæfed,   nymðe mec God scylde.
Ne meahte ic æt hilde   mid Hruntinge
wiht gewyrcan,   þeah þæt wæpen duge;
ac me geuðe   ylda Waldend
þæt ic on wage geseah   wlitig | hangian   [f.169v]
ealdsweord eacen   —oftost wisode
winigea leasum—   þæt ic ðy wæpne gebræd.
Oflsoh ða æt þære sæcce,   þa me sæl ageald,
huses hyrdas.   Þa þæt hildebil
forbarn, brogdenmæl,   swa þæt blod gesprang,
hatost heaþoswata.   Ic þæt hilt þanan
feondum ætferede;   fyrendæda wræc,
deaðcwealm Denigea,   swa hit gedefe wæs.
Ic hit þe þonne gehate,   þæt þu on Heorote most
sorhleas swefan   mid þinra secga gedryht,
ond þegna gehwylc   þinra leoda,
duguðe ond iogoþe,   þæt þu him ondrædan ne þearft,
þeoden Scyldinga,   on þa healfe,
aldorbealu eorlum,   swa þu ær dydest.'
Ða wæs gylden hilt   gamelum rince,
harum hildfruman   on hand gyfen,
enta ærgeweorc;   hit on æht gehwearf
æfter deofla hryre   Denigea frean,
wundorsmiþa geweorc;   ond þa þas worold ofgeaf
gromheort guma,   Godes andsaca,
morðres scyldig,   ond his modor eac;
on geweald gehwearf   woroldcyninga
ðæm selestan   be sæm tweonum   [f.170r]
ðara þe on Scedenigge   sceattas dælde.
Hroðgar maðelode,   hylt sceawode,
ealde lafe,   on ðæm wæs or writen
fyrngewinnes,   syðþan flod ofsloh,
gifen geotende   giganta cyn—
frecne geferdon;   þæt wæs fremde þeod
ecean Dryhtne;   him þæs endelean
þurh wæteres wylm   Waldend sealde.
Swa wæs on ðæm scennum   sciran goldes

fearsome for the eorls and the lady with them,
a horrible sight; men looked at it.
XXIIII Beowulf spoke, son of Ecgtheow:
'Indeed, son of Healfdene, man of the Scyldings,
we have brought thee gladly, as a sign of glory,
these sea-spoils, which thou lookest on here.
Not easily did I survive with my life
the battle under the water; venture upon the deed
in adversity; immediately would
the battle have ended, if God had not protected me.
I could achieve nothing in the battle with Hrunting,
although that weapon may be good;
but the Ruler of men granted me
that I should see | hanging handsome on the wall [f.169v]
a huge old sword —he has very often guided
the friendless— so that I drew the weapon.
Then, in the conflict I killed the house guardians,
when opportunity permitted me. Then that battle-brand,
the patterned blade, burned away, as their blood burst out,
hottest of battle-gore. Thence from the foes I
carried away that hilt; I avenged the wicked deeds,
the slaughter of the Danes, as it was seemly.
So, I promise thee that in Heorot thou mayst
sleep free from care amid thy band of men,
and for each one of the thanes among thy people,
veterans and youths, that thou needst not dread
deadly evil for thy warriors from that quarter,
as thou didst before, prince of Scyldings.'
Then was the golden hilt given into the hand
of the old warrior, the grizzled war-leader —
the ancient work of giants; it passed into the possession
of the lord of the Danes, after the fall of fiends,
the work of wondrous smiths; and when
the hostile-hearted creature, God's adversary,
guilty of murder, gave up this world, and his mother too,
it passed into the power of the best
of earthly kings between the | seas [f.170r]
of those who shared out treasure in Scandinavia.
  Hrothgar spoke, examined the hilt,
the old heirloom, on which was engraved the origin
of the ancient strife, when the flood,
the rushing ocean, destroyed the race of giants —
they fared terribly; that people was estranged
from the eternal Lord; the Ruler gave them
final retribution for that by the water's surging.
Thus on the metal plates of shining gold

þurh runstafas rihte gemearcod,
geseted ond gesæd hwam þæt sweord geworht,
irena cyst ærest wære,
wreoþenhilt ond wyrmfah. Ða se wisa spræc
sunu Healfdenes —swigedon ealle—:
'Þæt, la, mæg secgan se þe soð ond riht
fremeð on folce, feor eal gemon,
eald eþelweard, þæt ðes eorl wære
geboren betera! Blæd is aræred
geond widwegas, wine min Beowulf,
ðin ofer þeoda gehwylce. Eal þu hit geþyldum healdest,
mægen mid modes snyttrum. Ic þe sceal mine gelæstan
freode, swa wit furðum spræcon. Ðu scealt to frofre weorþan
eal langtwidig leodum þinum, |
hæleðum to helpe. [f.170v]
Ne wearð Heremod swa
eaforum Ecgwelan, Ar-Scyldingum;
ne geweox he him to willan, ac to wælfealle
ond to deaðcwalum Deniga leodum;
breat bolgenmod beodgeneatas,
eaxlgesteallan, oþþæt he ana hwearf,
mære þeoden mondreamum from.
Ðeah þe hine mihtig God mægenes wynnum,
eafeþum stepte, ofer ealle men
forð gefremede, hwæþere him on ferhþe greow
breosthord blodreow. Nallas beagas geaf
Denum æfter dome; dreamleas gebad
þæt he þæs gewinnes weorc þrowade,
leodbealo longsum. Ðu þe lær be þon,
gumcyste ongit! Ic þis gid be þe
awræc wintrum frod.
Wundor is to secganne,
hu mihtig God manna cynne
þurh sidne sefan snyttru bryttað,
eard ond eorlscipe; he ah ealra geweald.
Hwilum he on lufan læteð hworfan
monnes modgeþonc mæran cynnes,
seleð him on eþle eorþan wynne
to healdanne hleoburh wera, |
gedeð him swa gewealdene worolde dælas, [f.171r]
side rice, þæt he his selfa ne mæg
for his unsnyttrum ende geþencean.
Wunað he on wiste; no hine wiht dweleð
adl ne yldo, ne him inwitsorh
on sefa[n] sweorceð, ne gesacu ohwær
ecghete eoweð, ac him eal worold

was it correctly marked in runic letters,
set down and stated for whom that sword,
best of weapons, had first been wrought,
with twisted hilt and serpent shapes. Then spoke the wise
son of Healfdene —all were silent—:
'Lo! one may say, who effects truth and justice
among the people, remembers everything from the past,
an old guardian of the homeland, that this eorl was born
a better man! Through distant regions
thy renown is exalted, Beowulf, my friend,
over each people. Thou preservest all with patience,
thy might with wisdom of mind. I shall fulfil
my pledge, as we two spoke earlier. Thou shalt become
an entirely long-lasting comfort to thy people, | [f.170v]
a help to warriors.
Not so was Heremod
to Ecgwela's sons, the Honour-Scyldings;
he did not grow up as a joy to them, but for the slaughter
and death of the Danish people;
enraged, he slew his table companions,
his comrades, until he turned, alone,
the famous prince, from human joys.
Although mighty God exalted him
by the joys of power, over all men
advanced him, yet, in him there grew
a bloodthirsty heart. He never gave rings
to the Danes in pursuit of glory; joyless he lived on
to suffer the misery of that strife,
a prolonged affliction to his people. Teach thyself by that,
understand virtue! I tell this tale for thee,
wise with years.
It is wondrous to tell
how mighty God, because of his great spirit,
distributes wisdom among mankind,
land, and nobility; he possesses power over all.
Sometimes he allows the mind of a man
of famous race to wander in delight,
gives him in his native land the joys
of domain, a stronghold of men to possess; [f.171r]
makes parts of the world, a wide kingdom,
so subject to him, that he himself through his folly
cannot conceive of an end to it.
He dwells in prosperity; nothing afflicts him,
neither sickness nor age; nor does evil anxiety
darken his mind, nor enmity anywhere
show deadly hostility, but the whole world

wendeð on willan; he þæt wyrse ne con,
XXV oðþæt him on innan oferhygda dæl
weaxe[ð] ond wridað; þonne se weard swefeð,
sawele hyrde; bið se slæp to fæst,
bisgum gebunden, bona swiðe neah,
se þe of flanbogan fyrenum sceoteð.
Þonne bið on hreþre under helm drepen
biteran stræle —him bebeorgan ne con—
wom wundorbebodum wergan gastes:
þinceð him to lytel þæt he lange heold,
gytsað gromhydig, nallas on gylp seleð
fæ[tt]e beagas, ond he þa forðgesceaft
forgyteð ond forgymeð, þæs þe him ær God sealde,
wuldres | Waldend, weorðmynda dæl. [f.171v]
Hit on endestæf eft gelimpeð
þæt se lichoma læne gedreoseð,
fæge gefealleð; fehð oþer to,
se þe unmurnlice madmas dæleþ,
eorles ærgestreon, egesan ne gymeð.
Bebeorh þe ðone bealonið, Beowulf leofa,
secg betsta, ond þe þæt selre geceos,
ece rædas; oferhyda ne gym,
mære cempa! Nu is þines mægnes blæd
ane hwile; eft sona bið
þæt þec adl oððe ecg eafoþes getwæfeð,
oððe fyres feng oððe flodes wylm,
oððe gripe meces oððe gares fliht,
oððe atol yldo; oððe eagena bearhtm
forsiteð ond forsworceð. Semninga bið
þæt ðec, dryhtguma, deað oferswyðeð.
Swa ic Hring-Dena hund missera
weold under wolcnum, ond hig wigge beleac
manigum mægþa geond þysne middangeard,
æscum ond ecgum, þæt ic me ænigne
under swegles begong gesacan ne tealde.
Hwæt, me þæs on eþle edwend[e]n cwom,
gyrn æfter gomene, seoþðan Grendel wearð,
ealdgewinna, ingenga min; |
ic þære socne singales wæg [f.172r]
modceare micle. Þæs sig Metode þanc,
ecean Dryhtne, þæs ðe ic on aldre gebad
þæt ic on þone hafelan heorodreorigne
ofer eald gewin eagum starige!
Ga nu to setle, symbelwynne dreoh
wiggeweorþad; unc sceal worn fela
maþma gemænra siþðan morgen bið.'

goes according to his wish. He knows nothing worse,
XXV until within him a measure of arrogance
grows and flourishes; when the guardian sleeps,
the soul's keeper; that sleep is too sound,
bound in cares, with the slayer very close at hand,
who wickedly shoots from his bow.
Then, beneath his helmet, he is struck in the heart
by the sharp arrow —unable to protect himself—
by the perverse promptings of the evil spirit;
what he long possessed seems to him too paltry;
he covets fiercely, never proudly gives
gold-plated rings, and forgets and neglects
the destiny which God, the Ruler | of glory, [f.171v]
formerly gave him, his share of honours.
In the end it comes to pass
that the transitory body declines,
falls fated to die; another man takes possession,
who ungrudgingly shares out treasures,
the eorl's ancient wealth, heeds not fear.
Guard against that pernicious evil, dear Beowulf,
best of men; and choose the better,
eternal gains; be not intent on pride,
famous warrior! Now the glory of thy power
endures a while; yet soon it shall be
that disease or sword deprives thee of strength,
or fire's grasp, or flood's surge,
or sword's grip, or spear's flight,
or terrible old age, or brightness of eyes
fails and grows dim. Presently, it will be
that death overpowers thee, noble man.
Thus have I ruled the Ring-Danes fifty years
beneath the skies, protected them in war
against many nations throughout this earth,
with spear and sword, so that I did not consider
that I had any adversary beneath the expanse of heaven.
Indeed, a reversal came upon me in my land,
grief after joy, when Grendel,
ancient adversary, became an invader;
great sorrow of mind I | continually bore [f.172r]
from his persecution. For that, thanks be to God,
eternal Lord, for what I experienced in life,
that with my eyes I gaze upon that head
blood-stained from battle after the old struggle!
Go now to thy seat, relish the joy of feasting,
exalted by battle; a great many treasures we two
shall share between us when morning comes.'

Geat wæs glædmod,   geong sona to
setles neosan,   swa se snottra heht.
Þa wæs eft swa ær   ellenrofum
fletsittendum   fægere gereorded
niowan stefne.   Nihthelm geswearc
deorc ofer dryhtgumum.   Duguð eal aras;
wolde blondenfeax   beddes neosan,
gamela Scylding.   Geat unigmetes wel,
rofne randwigan   restan lyste;
sona him seleþegn   siðes wergum,
feorrancundum   forð wisade,
se for andrysnum   ealle beweote[d]e
þegnes þearfe,   swylce þy dogore
heaþoliðende   habban scoldon.
Reste hine þa rumheort;   reced hliuade
geap ond goldfah;   gæst inne swæf,
oþþæt hrefn blaca   heofones wynne
bliðheort bodode. | Ða com beorht scacan   [f.172v]
[scima ofer sceadwa];   scaþan onetton,
wæron æþelingas   eft to leodum
fuse to faren[n]e;   wolde feor þanon
cuma collenferhð   ceoles neosan.
Heht þa se hearda   Hrunting beran
sunu Ecglafes,   heht his sweord niman,
leoflic iren;   sægde him þæs leanes þanc,
cwæð, he þone guðwine   godne tealde,
wigcræftigne,   nales wordum log
meces ecge;   þæt wæs modig secg.
Ond þa siðfrome,   searwum gearwe
wigend wæron;   eode weorð Denum
æþeling to yppan,   þær se oþer wæs,
h[æ]le hildedeor   Hroðgar grette.
XXVI Beowulf maþelode,   bearn Ecgþeowes;
'Nu we sæliðend   secgan wyllað,
feorran cumene,   þæt we fundiaþ
Higelac secan.   Wæron her tela,
willum bewenede;   þu us wel dohtest.
Gif ic þonne on eorþan   owihte mæg
þinre modlufan   maran tilian,
gumena dryhtne,   ðonne ic gyt dyde,
guðgeweorca,   ic beo gearo sona.
Gif ic þæt ge | fricge   ofer floda begang,   [f.173r]
þæt þec ymbsittend   egesan þywað,
swa þec hetende   hwilum dydon,
ic ðe þusenda   þegna bringe,
hæleþa to helpe.   Ic on Higelace wat,

The Geat was glad at heart, straightway he went
to seek his seat, as the wise one enjoined.
Then, as before, for those strong in courage
sitting in hall, was a feast finely prepared
anew. The cover of night grew dark
over the warriors. The retainers all rose;
the grey-haired one, the old Scylding,
wished to seek his bed. Greatly did the Geat,
that brave shield-warrior, desire to rest;
straightway the chamberlain, who in courtesy
attended to all the needs of a thane, such things
as it was fitting for seafaring warriors
come from afar in that day to have,
guided him forth, weary with his exploit.
The great-hearted one rested; the building towered,
spacious and gold-adorned; the guest slept within,
until the black raven, joyful in heart,
heralded heaven's joy. | Then came the bright light [f.172v]
[radiance following shadows]; the warriors hastened,
the æthelings were eager to go again
to their people; brave in heart, the visitor
wished to seek his ship far thence.
Then the brave son of Ecglaf ordered Hrunting
to be brought, enjoined him to take his sword,
that precious weapon; Beowulf expressed thanks to him
for that loan, said he considered it a good war-friend,
strong in battle; in his words found no fault at all
with the sword's edge; that was a noble-minded man.
And when, eager to depart, the warriors were ready
in their armour, the ætheling honoured by the Danes
went to the dais, where the other was;
the warrior brave in battle greeted Hrothgar.
XXVI Beowulf spoke, son of Ecgtheow:
'Now we seafarers, come from afar,
wish to say that we are eager to go
to Hygelac. We have been entertained splendidly here,
as well as we might wish; thou hast treated us well.
If I can in anything on earth
earn more of thy heart's affection,
lord of men, than I have yet done,
I shall be ready at once for warlike deeds.
If beyond the sea's expanse I | learn [f.173r]
that neighbouring peoples threaten thee,
as enemies have done at times,
I shall bring thee a thousand thanes,
warriors to help. As for Hygelac, I know

Geata dryhten, þeah ðe he geong sy,
folces hyrde, þæt he mec fremman wile
w[o]rdum ond weorcum, þæt ic þe wel herige
ond þe to geoce garholt bere,
mægenes fultum, þær ðe bið manna þearf.
Gif him þonne Hreþri[c] to hofum Geata
geþinge[ð], þeodnes bearn, he mæg þær fela
freonda findan; feorcyþðe beoð
selran gesohte þæm þe him selfa deah.'
Hroðgar maþelode him on andsware:
'Þe þa wordcwydas wigtig Drihten
on sefan sende; ne hyrde ic snotorlicor
on swa geongum feore guman þingian.
Þu eart mægenes strang, ond on mode frod,
wis wordcwida! Wen ic talige,
gif þæt gegangeð þæt ðe gar nymeð,
hild heorugrimme Hreþles eaferan,
adl oþðe iren ealdor ðinne,
folces hyrde, ond þu þin feorh hafast,
þæt þe Sæ | -Geatas selran næbben [f.173v]
to geceosenne cyning ænigne,
hordweard hæleþa, gyf þu healdan wylt
maga rice. Me þin modsefa
licað leng swa wel, leofa Beo[w]ulf.
Hafast þu gefered, þæt þam folcum sceal,
Geata leodum ond Gar-Denum
sib gemæn[e], on sacu restan,
inwitniþas, þe hie ær drugon,
wesan þenden ic wealde widan rices
maþmas gemæne, manig oþerne
godum gegret[t]an ofer ganotes bæð;
sceal hringnaca ofer hea[f]u bringan
lac ond luftacen. Ic þa leode wat
ge wið feond ge wið freond fæste geworhte,
æghwæs untæle ealde wisan.'
Ða git him eorla hleo inne gesealde,
mago Healfdenes, maþmas twelfe,
het [h]in[e] mid þæm lacum leode swæse
secean on gesyntum, snude eft cuman.
Gecyste þa cyning æþelum god,
þeoden Scyldinga ðegn betstan
ond be healse genam; hruron him tearas
blondenfeaxum. Him wæs bega wen,
ealdum, in | frodum, oþres swiðor, [f.173r]
þæt h[i]e seoðða[n no] geseon moston,
modige on meþle. [W]æs him se man to þon leof,

that the lord of the Geats, his people's guardian,
though he be young, that he will support me
by words and deeds, that I may honour thee
and bring to thy help a forest of spears,
the support of strength, where thou hast need of men.
If Hrethric, the prince's son, decides to go
to the court of the Geats, he may find
many friends there; distant lands are more
fittingly visited by one who is himself of worth.'
   Hrothgar spoke to him in answer:
'The wise Lord has sent those words
into thy mind; never have I heard a man
so young of age speak more wisely.
Thou art strong of might and wise in mind,
sensible in speech. I think it likely,
if it happens that the spear takes
the son of Hrethel, fierce battle,
sickness or sword, takes thy prince,
the people's guardian, and thou hast thy life,
that the | Sea-Geats will not have [f.173v]
any better king to choose,
treasure-guardian of warriors, if thou wilt rule
thy kinsmen's kingdom. Thy spirit pleases me
better as time goes on, dear Beowulf.
Thou hast brought it to pass between the nations,
the people of the Geats and the Spear-Danes,
that peace shall be shared and strife cease,
enmities which they formerly endured;
while I rule over this wide realm,
treasures shall be shared; many a man
greet another with gifts over the gannet's bath;
the ring-prowed ship shall bring over the seas
gifts and tokens of love. I know that the people
are staunch in disposition towards both foe and friend,
blameless in every respect, according to the old custom.'
   Then the son of Healfdene, protector of eorls,
gave him within the hall twelve treasures;
enjoined him with those gifts to go
to his dear people in safety, return quickly.
Then the king, of noble descent, the prince
of the Scyldings, kissed the best of thanes,
and clasped him round the neck; tears fell
from him, the grey-haired man. Of two things he had
expectation, old | and very wise, one more especially, [f.174r]
that they would never have the opportunity to see each other again,
as brave men in council. The man was so dear to him

þæt he þone breostwylm   forberan ne mehte;
ac him on hreþre   hygebendum fæst
æfter deorum men   dyrne langað
beorn wið blode.   Him Beowulf þanan,
guðrinc goldwlanc   græsmoldan træd
since hremig;   sægenga bad
age[n]dfrean,   se þe on ancre rad.
Þa wæs on gange   gifu Hroðgares
oft geæhted;   þæt wæs an cyning
æghwæs orleahtre,   oþþæt hine yldo benam
mægenes wynnum,   se þe oft manegum scod.
XXVII Cwom þa to flode   felamodigra
hægstealdra [heap];   hringnet bæron,
locene leoðosyrcan.   Landweard onfand
eftsið eorla,   swa he ær dyde;
no he mid hearme   of hliðes nosan |
gæs[tas] grette,   ac him togeanes rad, [f.174v]
cwæð þæt wilcuman   Wedera leodum
scaþan scirhame   to scipe foron.
Þa wæs on sande   sægeap naca
hladen herewædum,   hringedstefna,
mearum ond maðmum;   mæst hlifade
ofer Hroðgares   hordgestreonum.
He þæm batwearde   bunden golde
swurd gesealde,   þæt he syðþan wæs
on meodubence   maþm[e] þy weorþr[a],
yrfelafe.   Gewat him on nac[a]
drefan deop wæter;   Dena land ofgeaf.
Þa wæs be mæste   merehrægla sum,
segl sale fæst;   sundwudu þunede.
No þær wegflotan   wind ofer yðum
siðes getwæfde;   sægenga for,
fleat famigheals   forð ofer yðe,
bundenstefna   ofer brimstreamas,
þæt hie Geata clifu   ongitan meahton,
cuþe næssas;   ceol up geþrang,
lyftgeswenced   on lande stod.
Hraþe wæs æt | holme   hyðweard geara, [f.175r]
se þe ær lange tid   leofra manna
fus æt faroðe   feor wlatode;
sælde to sande   sidfæþme scip
onc[e]rbendum fæst,   þy læs hym yþa ðrym
wudu wynsuman   forwrecan meahte.
Het þa up beran   æþelinga gestreon,
frætwe ond fætgold;   næs him feor þanon
to gesecanne   sinces bryttan,

that he could not restrain his surging emotion;
but in his breast, fast in the bonds of his heart,
a hidden longing for the dear man
burned in his blood. Thence Beowulf,
a warrior proudly gold-adorned, walked on the grassy earth,
exulting in treasure; the ship,
which rode at anchor, awaited its owner and lord.
Then, on the way, Hrothgar's gift
was often praised; that was one king
blameless in every respect, until old age, which has often
harmed many, deprived him of the joys of his strength.
XXVII Then to the flood came the band of very brave
young warriors; they wore mail-coats,
interlocked mail-shirts. The coastguard perceived
the return of the eorls, as erstwhile he did;
he did not greet the guests with insult | [f.174v]
from the cliff's top, but rode towards them,
said that the men in bright armour going down to the ship
would be welcome to the people of the Weders.
Then was the spacious vessel on the sand
laden with battle-gear, the ring-prowed ship,
with horses and treasures; the mast towered
over Hrothgar's hoarded wealth.
Beowulf gave the boat-keeper a sword
bound with gold, so that afterwards he was the more
esteemed on the mead-bench because of that treasure,
the heirloom. He embarked on the ship,
to plough the deep water; left the land of the Danes.
Then to the mast, a sea-cloth, a sail,
was bound by a rope; the timbers creaked.
The wind over the waves did not hinder the wave-
floater from its journey; the ship went its way,
foamy-necked floated forth over the wave,
with bound prow over the sea-streams,
until they could see the cliffs of the Geats,
the familiar headlands; the ship drove on ashore;
wind-battered, it stood on land.
Swiftly at the | water's edge was the harbour-guard ready, [f.175r]
he who for a long time had eagerly looked
far out at the sea for the dear men;
he moored the broad-bosomed ship to the sand,
fast by its anchor-ropes, lest the force of the waves
should drive to destruction the handsome wooden craft.
Then he ordered the æthelings' treasure to be carried up,
adornments and plated gold; it was not far thence
for him to go to Hygelac, son of Hrethel,

Higelac Hreþling, þær æt ham wunað
selfa mid gesiðum sæwealle neah.
Bold wæs betlic, bregorof cyning,
hea[h on] healle, Hygd swiðe geong,
wis welþungen, þeah ðe wintra lyt
under burhlocan gebiden hæbbe,
Hæreþes dohtor; næs hio hnah swa þeah,
ne to gneað gifa Geata leodum,
maþmgestreona. Modþryðo wæg,
fremu folces cwen, firen' ondrysne;
nænig þæt dorste deor geneþan
swæsra gesiða, nefne sinfrea,
þæt hire an dæges eagum starede,
ac him wælbende | weotode tealde [f.175v]
handgewriþene: hraþe seoþðan wæs
æfter mundgripe mece geþinged,
þæt hit sceadenmæl scyran moste,
cwealmbealu cyðan. Ne bið swylc cwenlic þeaw
idese to efnanne, þeah ðe hio ænlicu sy,
þætte freoðuwebbe feores onsæce
æfter ligetorne leofne mannan.
Huru þæt onhohsnod[e] Hem[m]inges mæg:
ealodrincende oðer sædan,
þæt hio leodbealewa læs gefremede,
inwitniða, syððan ærest wearð
gyfen goldhroden geongum cempan,
æðelum diore, syððan hio Offan flet
ofer fealone flod be fæder lare
siðe gesohte. Ðær hio syððan well
in gumstole, gode mære,
lifgesceafta lifigende breac;
hiold heahlufan wið hæleþa brego,
ealles moncynnes mine gefræge
þ[one] selestan bi sæm tweonum,
eormencynnes; forðam Offa | wæs [f.176r]
geofum ond guðum, garcene man,
wide geweorðod, wisdome heold
eðel sinne. Þonon [E]om[e]r woc
hæleðum to helpe, Hem[m]inges mæg,
nefa Garmundes, niða cræftig.

XXVIII Gewat him ða se hearda mid his hondscole
sylf æfter sande sæwong tredan,
wide waroðas. Woruldcandel scan,
sigel suðan fus. Hi sið drugon,
elne geeodon to ðæs ðe eorla hleo,
bonan Ongenþeoes burgum in innan,

the bestower of treasure, where he dwelt at home,
himself with his companions, near the sea-cliff.
The building was magnificent, the king of princely valour,
exalted in the hall, Hygd very young,
wise, accomplished, although she, the daughter
of Hæreth, had lived few winters within
the enclosed stronghold; yet she was not niggardly,
nor, to the people of the Geats, too grudging of gifts,
costly treasures. Modthryth, an imperious
queen of the nation, committed terrible evil;
no brave man among the dear companions,
except her husband, dared venture to look
upon her with his eyes by day;
but [if he did] he would reckon deadly bonds, twisted by hand, [f.175v]
ordained for him: swiftly after his seizure
the sword was allotted for him,
so that the patterned blade had to settle the matter,
make known its deadly evil. No queenly custom that
for a woman to practise, though peerless she be,
that a peace-weaver should deprive a man
of life because of a fancied insult.
However, the kinsman of Hemming stopped that;
men at their ale-drinking told a different tale,
that she performed fewer evils on the people,
malicious acts, as soon as she, gold-adorned,
noble in lineage, had been given in marriage
to the young warrior, when she sought
Offa's hall by her father's counsel
over the pale sea. There, afterwards,
she used her fortunes well upon the throne,
famed for her goodness, while still alive;
she held deep love towards the prince of heroes,
who was of all mankind, as I have heard,
the best between the seas
of the race of men, for Offa | was [f.176r]
a skilled spearman, widely honoured
for gifts and victories, with wisdom ruled
his homeland. From him was born Eomær,
help to warriors, kinsman of Hemming,
grandson of Garmund, powerful in battle.

XXVIII Then the hardy warrior with his band of companions
himself went along the sand, treading the beach,
the wide shores. The world's candle shone,
the sun hastening from the south. They made their way,
went eagerly to where they had heard tell
that the protector of eorls, the slayer of Ongentheow,

geongne guðcyning godne gefrunon
hringas dælan. Higelace wæs
sið Beowulfes snude gecyðed,
þæt ðær on worðig wigendra hleo,
lindgestealla lifigende cwom,
heaðolaces hal to hofe gongan.
Hraðe wæs gerymed, swa se rica bebead,
feðegestum flet innanweard.
Gesæt þa wið sylfne se ða sæcce genæs,
mæg wið mæge, | siððan mandryhten [f.176v]
þurh hleoðorcwyde holdne gegrette,
meaglum wordum. Meoduscencum hwearf
geond þæt [heal]reced Hæreðes dohtor,
lufode þa leode, liðwæge bær
hæ[leð]um to handa. Higelac ongan
sinne geseldan in sele þam hean
fægere fricgean —hyne fyrwet bræc
hwylce Sæ-Geata siðas wæron:
'Hu lomp eow on lade, leofa Biowulf,
þa ðu færinga feorr gehogodest
sæcce secean ofer sealt wæter,
hilde to Hiorote? Ac ðu Hroðgare
wi[d]cuðne wean wihte gebettest,
mærum ðeodne? Ic ðæs modceare
sorhwylmum seað, siðe ne truwode
leofes mannes; ic ðe lange bæd
þæt ðu þone wælgæst wihte ne grette,
lete Suð-Dene sylfe geweorðan
guðe wið Grendel. Gode ic þanc secge
þæs ðe ic ðe gesundne geseon moste.'
Biowulf maðelode, bearn Ecgðioes: [f.177r]
'Þæt is undyrne, dryhten Higelac,
[micel] gemeting, monegum fira,
hwyl[c orleg] hwil uncer Grendles
wearð on ðam wange, þær he worna fela
Sige-Scyldingum sorge gefremede,
yrmðe to aldre; ic ðæt eall gewræc,
swa begylpan [ne] þearf Grendles maga
[æ]n[ig] ofer eorðan uhthlem þone,
se ðe lengest leofað laðan cynnes,
f[acne] bifongen. Ic ðær furðum cwom
to ðam hringsele Hroðgar gretan;
sona me se mæra mago Healfdenes,
syððan he modsefan minne cuðe,
wið his sylfes sunu setl getæhte.
Weorod wæs on wynne; ne seah ic widan feorh

the worthy young war-king, in the stronghold
was sharing out rings. Beowulf's journey
was quickly announced to Hygelac,
that there in the precinct the protector of warriors,
his shield-companion, had come alive
to the court, unscathed from the battle.
Swiftly was the hall cleared within
for the foot-guests, as the ruler commanded.
Then he who survived the strife sat opposite the king himself,
kinsman facing kinsman, | after he had greeted [f.176v]
his liege lord in loyal ceremonious speech,
with solemn words. Hæreth's daughter moved about
through that hall with mead-cups,
loved the people, bore the cup containing drink
to the hands of the warriors. Hygelac began
courteously to question his companion
in the lofty hall —curiosity pressed him to know
what the adventures of the Sea-Geats had been:
'How fared ye on the journey, dear Beowulf,
when thou didst suddenly resolve to seek
a conflict far off, over the salt wave,
battle at Heorot? Hast thou remedied in any way
the widely-known woes of Hrothgar,
the famous prince? For that, I was troubled in mind
with surging sorrows, trusted not the venture
of my dear man; I long entreated thee
that thou wouldst not at all attack the murderous creature,
allow the South-Danes themselves to settle
their fight with Grendel. I give thanks to God
that I was allowed to see thee safe.'
Beowulf spoke, son of Ecgtheow: | [f.177r]
'That great encounter, lord Hygelac,
is manifest to many men,
what period of conflict there was between Grendel and me
in that place, where he had brought about
a great many sorrows for the Victory-Scyldings,
miseries for ever; I avenged all that,
in such a way that none of Grendel's kin on earth
need boast about that uproar at night,
whoever, encompassed by crime, lives longest
of the loathsome race. There I went first
to the ring-hall to greet Hrothgar;
straightway the famous son of Healfdene,
when he knew my mind,
allotted me a seat with his own sons.
His company was joyous; never have I seen

under heofones hwealf   healsittendra
medudream maran.   Hwilum mæru cwen,
friðusibb folca   flet eall geondhwearf,
bædde byre geonge;   oft hio beahwriðan
secge [sealde] | ær hie to setle geong. [f.177v]
Hwilum for [d]uguðe   dohtor Hroðgares
eorlum on ende   ealuwæge bær,
þa ic Freaware   fletsittende
nemnan hyrde,   þær hio [næ]gled sinc
hæleðum sealde.   Sio gehaten [is],
geong goldhroden,   gladum suna Frodan;
[h]afað þæs geworden   wine Scyldinga,
rices hyrde,   ond þæt ræd talað
þæt he mid ðy wife   wælfæhða dæl,
sæcca gesette.   Oft seldan hwær
æfter leodhryre   lytle hwile
bongar bugeð,   þeah seo bryd duge.
   Mæg þæs þonne ofþyncan   ðeod[ne] Heaðo-Beardna
ond þegna gehwam   þara leoda,
þonne he mid fæmnan   on flett gæð,
dryhtbearn Dena   —duguða biwenede.
On him gladiað   gomelra lafe,
heard ond hringmæl   Heaðabear[d]na gestreon
þenden hie ðam wæpnum   wealdan moston,
[XXVIIII-XXX] oððæt hie forlæddan   to ðam lindplegan
swæse gesiðas   ond hyra sylfra feorh.
Þonne cwið æt beore   se ðe beah | gesyhð, [f.178r]
eald æscwiga,   se ðe eall ge[m]a[n],
garcwealm gumena   —him bið grim sefa—
onginneð geomormod   geong[um] cempan
þurh hreðra gehygd   higes cunnian,
wigbealu weccean,   ond þæt word acwyð:
'Meaht ðu, min wine,   mece gecnawan,
þone þin fæder   to gefeohte bær
under heregriman   hindeman siðe,
dyre iren,   þær hyne Dene slogon,
weoldon wælstowe   syððan Wiðergyld læg,
æfter hæleþa hryre,   hwate Scyldungas?
Nu her þara banena   byre nathwylces
frætwum hremig   on flet gæð,
morðres gylpe[ð],   ond þone maðþum byreð,
þone þe ðu mid rihte   rædan sceoldest.'
Manað swa ond myndgað   mæla gehwylce
sarum wordum,   oððæt sæl cymeð
þæt se fæmnan þegn   fore fæder dædum
æfter billes bite   blodfag swefeð,

under heaven's vault among men sitting in the hall
greater joy over mead. At times the famous queen,
the people's pledge of peace, went throughout the hall,
urged on the young men; often she gave a circlet
to some man, | ere she went to her seat. [f.177v]
At times, Hrothgar's daughter bore the ale-cup
before the retainers, to the eorls in turn;
then I heard those sitting in the hall call her Freawaru,
where she gave the studded precious vessel
to the warriors. She is promised,
young and gold-adorned, to the gracious son of Froda;
it has been settled by the lord of the Scyldings,
the guardian of the realm, and he considers it wise policy,
that with this woman he may settle a great number
of deadly feuds and conflicts. As a rule,
after the fall of a prince the deadly spear rests only
for a short while anywhere, even though the bride may be good.
It may then displease the prince of the Heathobards
and each of the thanes of that people
when he, the wedding-attendant of the Danes —who
were nobly entertained— enters the hall with the woman.
On them shine old heirlooms,
hard and ring-patterned, treasure of the Heathobards,
while they were able to wield those weapons,
[XXVIIII–XXX] ere they led to destruction in shield-play
their dear companions and their own lives.
Then at the beer-drinking an old spear-warrior,
who | sees a ring-hilt, remembers it all, [f.178r]
the spear-death of men —his heart is grim—
begins, sad of mind, to test a young warrior's
spirit by the musings of his heart,
to arouse evil strife, and utters these words:
'Canst thou, my friend, recognize the sword,
the precious blade, which thy father bore to battle,
when he was helmed for his last expedition,
where the Danes slew him,
the valiant Scyldings held the field,
when Withergyld lay low, after the fall of warriors?
Now someone here, a son of these slayers,
exulting in adornments, walks in the hall,
boasts of the murder, and bears the treasure,
which thou shouldst rightly possess.'
Thus, each time he will urge and remind
with bitter words, until the time comes
when the woman's thane, because of his father's deeds,
after the sword-stroke sleeps blood-stained,

eldres scyldig; him se oðer þonan
losað | [li]figende, con him land geare. [f.178v]
Þonne bioð [ab]rocene on ba healfe
aðsweor*d* eorla; [syð]ðan Ingelde
weallað wælniðas, ond him wiflufan
æfter cearwælmum colran weorðað.
Þy ic Heaðobear[d]na hyldo ne telge,
dryhtsibbe dæl Denum unfæcne,
freondscipe fæstne.
Ic sceal forð sprecan
gen ymbe Grendel, þæt ðu geare cunne,
sinces brytta, to hwan syððan wearð
hondræs hæleða. Syððan heofones gim
glad ofer grundas gæst yrre cwom,
eatol æfengrom user neosan,
ðær we gesunde sæl weardodon.
Þær wæs Hondscio hil[d] onsæge,
feorhbealu fægum; he fyrmest læg,
gyrded cempa; him Grendel wearð,
mærum mag[u]þegne to muðbonan,
leofes mannes lic eall forswealg.
No ðy ær ut ða gen idelhende
bona blodigtoð, bealewa gemyndig,
of ðam goldsele gongan wolde;
ac he mægnes rof min costode, | [f.179r]
grapode gear[o]folm. Glof hangode
sid ond syllic, searobendum fæst;
sio wæs orðoncum eall gegyrwed
deofles cræftum ond dracan fellum.
He mec þær on innan unsynnigne,
dior dædfruma gedon wolde
manigra sumne; hyt ne mihte swa,
syððan ic on yrre uppriht astod.
To lang ys to reccenne, hu i[c ð]am leodsceaðan
yfla gehwylces [o]ndlean forgeald,
þær ic, þeoden min, þine leode
weorðode weorcum. He on weg losade,
lytle hwile lifwynna br[ea]c;
hwæþre him sio swiðre swaðe weardade
hand on Hiorte, ond he hean ðonan,
modes geomor meregrund gefeoll.
Me þone wælræs wine Scildunga
fættan golde fela leanode,
manegum maðmum, syððan mergen com,
ond we to symble geseten hæfdon.
Þær wæs gidd ond gleo; gomela | Scilding, [f.179v]

having forfeited life; the other thence
escapes | alive, knows the country well. [f.178v]
On both sides then there will be broken
the oath-swearing of eorls; in Ingeld
deadly hate well up, and love for a wife
grow cooler with surgings of sorrow.
Hence I consider not the loyalty of the Heathobards,
their share in the peace made by marriage, to be without deceit
towards the Danes, nor their friendship firm.
I shall speak further
about Grendel, that thou mayst know well, bestower of treasure,
what was the outcome of the hand-to-hand struggle
between the warriors. After heaven's gem
glided over the earth, the enraged creature came,
the dread night visitant, to seek us out,
where, safe and sound, we guarded the hall.
There was battle fatal to Hondscio,
deadly evil for the warrior fated to die; he fell first,
the girded warrior. Grendel devoured him,
the famous young thane,
swallowed up the body of the beloved man.
Yet, none the sooner would the slayer
with bloody teeth, bent on destruction,
go from the gold-hall empty-handed;
but he, strong of might, tested me, | [f.179r]
grasped me with ready hand. His glove hung,
broad and strange, secured by cunning clasps;
it was all contrived with ingenuity
by the devil's skill and with dragon skins.
Therein the fierce perpetrator of deeds
purposed to put me, though guiltless,
as one of many; he could not do so
when I stood upright in my wrath.
It is too long to tell how I repaid
the ravager of the people for every evil;
there, my prince, did I bring honour to thy people
with my deeds. He slipped away,
for a little while enjoyed life's joys;
but his right hand remained in Heorot
as his spoor, and he, abject, fleeing thence,
sad at heart, fell to the bottom of the mere.
The friend of the Scyldings rewarded me greatly
with plated gold for that mortal conflict,
with many treasures, when the morrow came,
and we had sat down to the feast.
There was song and musical entertainment; the old | Scylding, [f.179v]

felafricgende feorran rehte;
hwilum hildedeor hearpan wynne,
gome[n]wudu grette, hwilum gyd awræc
soð ond sarlic, hwilum syllic spell
rehte æfter rihte rumheort cyning;
hwilum eft ongan, eldo gebunden,
gomel guðwiga gioguðe cwiðan,
hildestrengo; hreðer [in]ne weoll,
þonne he wintrum frod worn gemunde.
Swa we þær inne andlangne dæg
niode naman, oððæt niht becwom
oðer to yldum. Þa wæs eft hraðe
gearo gyrnwræce Grendles modor,
siðode sorhfull; sunu deað fornam,
wighete Wedra. Wif unhyre
hyre bearn gewræc; beorn acwealde
ellenlice; þær wæs Æschere,
frodan fyrnwitan feorh uðgenge.
Noðer hy hine ne moston, syððan mergen cwom,
deaðwerigne Denia leode
bronde forbærnan, ne on bel hladan,
leofne mannan; | hio þæt lic ætbær [f.180r]
feondes fæð[mum un]der firgenstream.
Þæt wæs Hroðgar[e] hreowa tornost
þara þe leodfruman lange begeate.
Þa se ðeoden mec ðine life
healsode hreohmod, þæt ic on holma geþring
eorlscipe efnde, ealdre geneðde,
mærðo fremede; he me mede gehet.
Ic ða ðæs wælmes, þe is wide cuð,
grim[n]e gryrelicne grundhyrde fond.
Þær unc hwile wæs hand gemæne;
holm heolfre weoll, ond ic heafde becearf
in ðam [guð]sele Grendles modor
eacnum ecgum. Unsofte þonan
feorh oðferede; næs ic fæge þa gyt,
ac me eorla hleo eft gesealde
maðma menigeo, maga Healfdenes.
XXXI Swa se ðeodkyning þeawum lyfde.
Nealles ic ðam leanum forloren hæfde,
mægnes mede, ac he me | [maðma]s geaf, [f.180v]
sunu Healfdenes on [min]ne sylfes dom;
ða ic ðe, beorncyning, bringan wylle,
estum geywan. Gen is eall æt ðe
lissa gelong; ic lyt hafo
heafodmaga nefne, Hygelac, ðec.'

having learned of many things, recounted tales from long ago;
at times one brave in battle struck the harp in joy,
the delightful wood; at times he told a tale,
true and mournful; at times the great-hearted king
narrated a strange story according to right custom;
at times, again, fettered with age,
the old warrior began to lament his youth,
his battle-strength; his heart welled within him
when he, now old and wise, recalled many things.
Thus we took our pleasure there
the entire day till another night came
to men. Then swiftly again was
Grendel's mother ready for revenge for his injury;
she journeyed full of grief; Death had carried off her son,
the warlike enmity of the Weders. The monster-wife
avenged her child; killed a warrior
boldly; it was there from Æschere,
wise old counsellor, that life departed.
Not when morning came could the Danish people,
burn him up with fire,
death-weary, nor lay on the pyre
the dear man; | she carried off that body [f.180r]
in fiend's embrace beneath the mountain stream.
That was the most grievous of sorrows for Hrothgar,
of those that had long befallen the people's leader.
Then the prince, troubled in mind,
implored me by thy life, that in the water's tumult
I would perform a heroic deed, venture my life,
perform a glorious deed; he promised me reward.
Then, as is widely known, I found
the grim and terrible guardian of the deep.
There for a while we two fought hand to hand;
the water seethed with blood; and I cut off the head
of Grendel's mother in the battle-hall
with mighty sword-edge. With difficulty thence
I got away with my life; I was not doomed yet;
but the protector of eorls, the son of Healfdene,
again gave me a multitude of treasures.
XXXI Thus lived the people's king, with good customs.
I had lost none of the rewards,
the meed of my might, but he gave me | treasures [f.180v]
at my own choice, the son of Healfdene;
these I will bring to thee, warrior-king,
bestow with good will. On thee are still dependent
all favours; I have few
close kinsmen except for thee, Hygelac.'

Het ða in beran   eafor heafodsegn,
heaðosteapne helm,   hare byrnan,
guðsweord geatolic,   gyd æfter wræc:
'Me ðis hildesceorp   Hroðgar sealde,
snotra fengel;   sume worde het
þæt ic his ærest ðe   est gesægde;
cwæð þæt hyt hæfde   Hiorogar cyning,
leod Scyldunga   lange hwile;
no ðy ær suna sinum   syllan wolde,
hwatum Heorowearde,   þeah he him hold wære,
breostgewædu.   Bruc ealles well!'
Hyrde ic þæt þam frætwum   feower mearas
lungre, gelice   last weardode,
æppelfealuwe;   he him est geteah
meara ond maðma.   Swa sceal | mæg don,   [f.181r]
nealles inwitnet   oðrum bregdon
dyrnum cræfte,   deað ren[ian]
hondgesteallan.   Hygelace wæs
niða heardum   nefa swyðe hold,
ond gehwæðer oðrum   hroþra gemyndig.
Hyrde ic þæt he ðone healsbeah   Hygde gesealde,
wrætlicne wundurmaððum   ðone þe him Wealhðeo geaf,
ðeod[nes] dohtor,   þrio wicg somod
swancor ond sadolbeorht;   hyre syððan wæs
æfter beahðege   br[e]ost geweorðod.
Swa bealdode   bearn Ecgðeowes,
guma guðum cuð,   godum dædum,
dreah æfter dome;   nealles druncne slog
heorðgeneatas;   næs him hreoh sefa,
ac he mancynnes   mæste cræfte
ginfæstan gife   þe him God sealde,
heold hildedeor.   Hean wæs lange,
swa hyne Geata bearn   godne ne tealdon,
ne hyne on medobence   micles wyrðne | [f.181v]
drihten We[d]e[r]a   gedon wolde;
swyðe [wen]don,   þæt he sleac wære,
æðeling unfrom.   Edwenden cwom
tireadigum menn   torna gehwylces.
Het ða eorla hleo   in gefetian,
heaðorof cyning,   Hreðles lafe,
golde gegyrede;   næs mid Geatum ða
sincmaðþum selra   on sweordes had;
þæt he on Biowulfes   bearm alegde,
ond him gesealde   seofan þusendo,
bold ond bregostol.   Him wæs bam samod
on ðam leodscipe   lond gecynde,

Then he bade bring in the boar head-sign,
the helmet towering in battle, the grey byrny,
the splendid war-sword, then uttered speech:
'Hrothgar, the wise king, gave me
this battle-dress; he expressly commanded
that I should tell thee first of the gift of it;
he said that King Hiorogar,
a man of the Scyldings, had it a long time;
yet he would not give to his son,
bold Heoroweard, the breast-garment,
loyal though he were to him. Enjoy it well!
I have heard that four glossy-bay steeds,
swift and alike, followed in the track
of those adornments; he bestowed on him the gift
of horses and treasures. Thus must a | kinsman act, [f.181r]
never weave a net of malice for another,
prepare with secret cunning the death
of a close companion. To Hygelac,
hardy in battles, his nephew was very loyal
and each was mindful of the other's good.
I heard that he gave Hygd that neck-ring,
that splendid, wondrous jewel, that Wealhtheow,
a prince's daughter, gave him, together with three
graceful steeds with bright saddles; then was
her breast adorned, after receiving the ring.

Thus the son of Ecgtheow showed himself brave,
a man renowned in battles, doughty deeds,
acted in pursuit of glory; never at the drinking slew
his hearth-companions; his was no savage heart,
but, brave in battle, with the greatest strength
among mankind he kept the liberal gift which God
had granted him. Long was he despised,
for the sons of the Geats considered him worthless;
nor did the | lord of the Weders wish to make [f.181v]
him entitled to much at the mead-bench;
they very much thought that he was indolent,
a feeble prince. But there came a change
to the glorious man for every affliction.

Then the protector of eorls, bade bring in
the heirloom of Hrethel, the king brave in battle,
adorned with gold; with the Geats there was then
no finer treasure in the form of a sword;
that he laid in Beowulf's lap,
and gave him seven thousand [hides of land],
a hall, and princely throne. Both of them
by natural right possessed land in that country,

eard eðelriht, oðrum swiðor
side rice þam ðær selra wæs.
Eft þæt geiode ufaran dogrum
hildehlæmmum, syððan Hygelac læg
ond Hear[dr]ede hildemeceas
under bordhreoðan to bonan wurdon,
ða hyne gesohtan on sigeþeode
hearde hil[d]frecan, Heaðo-Scylfingas,
niða genægdan nefan Hererices,
syððan | Beowulfe br*a*de rice [f.181r]
on hand gehwearf. He geheold tela
fiftig wintra —wæs ða frod cyning,
eald eþelweard— oððæt an ongan
deorcum nihtum draca rics[i]an,
se ðe on hea*um* h*æþ*e hord beweotode,
stanbeorh stea*p*ne; stig under læg
eldum uncuð. Þær on innan giong
niða nathwylc, *se* [ðe] *neh* gefeng
hæðnum horde, hond [. . .]
since fahne; he þæt syððan [. . .]
þ[ea]*h* ð[e] *h*[e] slæpende besyre[d] *wu*[r]*de*
þeofes cræfte; þæt sie ðiod *onf*[an]*d*,
b*u*folc beorna, þæt he gebolge*n* wæs.
XXXII Nealles *mid* gewe*a*ldum wyrmhord a[b]ræ[c],
sylfes willum, se ðe him sare gesceod,
ac for þreanedlan þ[eow] nathwylces
hæleða bearna heteswengeas fle*a*h,
æ*rn*[e]*s* þearfa, ond ðær inne *f*eal[h],
secg synbysig. Sona [onfun]de
þæt [. . .] ðam gyste [gry]*re*br*oga* stod;
hwæðre [earm] sceapen [. . . . . | [f.182v]
. . . .] sceapen
[. . . . .] þa hyne se fæ*r* begeat.
Sincfæt [. . .] þær wæs swylcra fela
in ðam eorð[hu]se ærgestreona,
swa hy on geardagum gumena nathwylc,
eormenlafe æðelan cynnes,
þanchycgende þær gehydde,
deore maðmas. Ealle hie deað fornam
ærran mælum, ond s[e] an ða gen
leoda duguðe, se ðær lengest hwearf,
weard winegeomor, *w*ende þæs ylcan,
þæt he lytel fæc longgestreona
brucan moste. Beorh eallgearo
wunode on wonge wæteryðum neah,
niwe be næsse, nearocræftum fæst.

an ancestral domain, but rather to the other belonged
the broad kingdom, to the one whose rank was higher.
Afterwards it happened, in later days,
in the crashes of battle, after Hygelac lay dead
and battle-swords were slayers of Heardred,
beneath the shield's shelter,
when the warlike Scylfings, hardy warriors,
sought him out among his victorious people,
fiercely attacked the nephew of Hereric,
then the broad kingdom passed
into | Beowulf's hands. He ruled it well [f.181r]
for fifty years —he was then a wise king,
an old guardian of the homeland— until a certain one began
to hold sway in the dark nights, a dragon,
which, on a high heath, watched over a hoard
in a steep stone-barrow; a path lay beneath,
unknown to men. Into that place went
someone, who approached and grasped
the heathen hoard, with his hand [. . .]
a shining treasure; this he later [. . .]
although he had been tricked while sleeping
by the cunning of a thief; and thus the people
dwelling there discovered he was enraged.

XXXII Not of his own desire did he who had grievously
harmed him, deliberately break into the dragon's hoard;
but in dire distress the slave of someone
of the sons of men, had fled from hostile blows,
and in need of a dwelling, made his way there,
a guilty man. As soon as he discovered
that [....] in the intruder a great horror arose;
yet the | wretched [. [f.182v]
. . . .] created
[. . .] the sudden attack befell him.
There were many such precious vessels,
ancient treasures, in that earth-house,
as someone, in former times,
had thoughtfully hidden there,
the immense legacy of a noble race,
precious treasures. Death carried them all off
in former times, and still that one
veteran of the people, who lived longest there,
a guardian mourning for friends, expected the same,
that for a little time he might enjoy
the ancient treasures. A barrow fully ready
stood on open ground, near the sea-waves,
newly-made on the headland, inaccessibly secure.

Þær on innan bær eorlgestreona
hringa hyrde h[o]rdwyrðne dæl
fættan goldes; fea worda cwæð:
'Heald þu nu, hruse, nu hæleð ne m[o]st*o*n,
eorla æhte! Hwæt, hyt ær on ðe
gode begeaton; guðdeað fornam,
feorhbeal*o* frecne fyr[a] gehwylcne
leoda minra þa[r]a ðe þis [lif] ofgeaf:
gesawon seledream. | Nah, hwa sweord wege [f.183r]
oððe f[orð bere] fæted wæge,
dryncfæt deore; dug[uð] ellor s[c]eoc.
Sceal se hearda helm [hyr]stedgolde,
fætum befeallen; feormynd swefað,
þa ðe beadogriman bywan sceoldon;
ge swylce seo herepad, sio æt hilde gebad
ofer borda gebræc bite irena,
brosnað æfter beorne; ne mæg byrnan hring
æfter wigfruman wide feran
hæleðum be healfe. Næs hearpan wyn,
gomen gleobeames, ne god hafoc
geond sæl swingeð, ne se swifta mearh
burhstede beateð. Bealocwealm hafað
fela feorhcynna forð onsended.'
Swa giomormod giohðo mænde
an æfter eallum, unbliðe hwe[arf]
dæges ond nihtes, oððæt deaðes wylm
hran æt heortan. Hordwynne fond
eald uhtsceaða opene standan,
se ðe byrnende biorgas seceð,
nacod niðdraca, nihtes fleogeð
fyre befangen; hyne foldbuend |
[swiðe ondræ]*d*a[ð]. He gesecean sceall [f.183v]
h[o]r[d on h]rusan, þær he hæðen gold
warað wintrum frod; ne byð him wihte ðy sel.
Swa se ðeodsceaða þreo hund wintra
heold on hrusa[n] hordærna sum
eacencræftig, oððæt hyne an abealch
mon on mode; mandryhtne bær
fæted wæge, frioðowære bæd
hlaford sinne. Ða wæs hord rasod,
onboren beaga hord, bene getiðad
feasceaftum men; frea sceawode
fira fyrngeweorc forman siðe.
Þa se wyrm onwoc wroht wæs geniwad;
stonc ða æfter stane, stearcheort onfand
feondes fotlast; he to forð gestop

Into that place the keeper of rings had borne
a quantity of the noblemen's treasure
of plated gold; few words he spoke:
'Hold thou now, earth, now warriors may not,
the property of eorls! Lo, first from thee
worthy men obtained it; death in battle,
the terrible destroyer of life, has carried off
every one of my people who has left this life:
they have seen the last of the joy of hall. | I have none [f.183r]
to bear sword, or carry the plated cup,
precious drinking-vessel; the tried warriors have departed.
Now must the stout helmet, gold-adorned,
be shorn of its plating; the burnishers sleep in death,
who should polish the battle-masks;
and also the mail-coat, which endured in battle,
over the clash of shields, the cut of swords,
decays like its master; nor may the byrny's ring
journey widely behind the war-leader,
beside his warriors. There is no joy of the harp,
delight of the timbrel, nor does good hawk
fly through the hall, nor swift steed stamp
in the courtyard. Destructive death
has banished many of the living race.'
Thus, sad at heart, the sole survivor
spoke of sorrow, moved about joyless
by day and night, until death's surging
touched his heart. The old night-ravager,
the smooth-skinned malicious dragon, who seeks out barrows,
burning as he goes, who flies by night,
enveloped in flame, found the delightful hoard
standing open; earth-dwellers | greatly [f.183v]
fear him. He must needs seek out
a hoard in the earth, where, old in years,
he guards heathen gold; nor is he at all the better for it.
  So for three hundred years this ravager of a people
occupied a huge treasure-house in the earth,
until a certain man enraged him
in his heart; he carried to his lord
the gold-plated cup, and begged a peace-agreement
with his lord. Thus was the hoard explored,
the hoard of rings diminshed, his request granted
the wretched man; the lord looked at
the ancient work of men for the first time.
Then the serpent awoke; strife was renewed;
he moved swiftly along the rock, hard-hearted found
his enemy's track; he had stepped right up,

dyrnan cræfte   dracan heafde neah.
Swa mæg unfæge   eaðe gedigan
wean ond wræcsið,   se ðe Waldendes
hyldo gehealdeþ.   Hordweard sohte
georne æfter grunde;   wolde guman findan,
þone þe him on sweofote   sare geteode.
Hat ond hreohmod | hlæ[w] oft ymbehwearf   [f.184r]
ealne utanweardne   —ne ðær ænig mon
on þæ[m] westenne;   hwæðre [wiges] gefeh,
bea[duwe] weorces.   Hwilum on beorh æthwearf,
sincfæt sohte;   he þæt sona onfand
ðæt hæfde gumena sum   goldes gefandod,
heahgestreona.   Hordweard onbad
earfoðlice   oððæt æfen cwom;
wæs ða gebolgen   beorges hyrde,
wolde [s]e laða   lige forgyldan
drincfæt dyre.   Þa wæs dæg sceacen
wyrme on willan;   no on wealle læ[n]g
bidan wolde,   ac mid bæle for,
fyre gefysed.   Wæs se fruma egeslic
leodum on lande,   swa hyt lungre wearð
on hyra sincgifan   sare geendod.
XXXIII Ða se gæst ongan   gledum spiwan,
beorht hofu bærnan,   bryneleoma stod
eldum on andan;   no ðær aht cwices
lað lyftfloga   læfan | wolde.   [f.184v]
Wæs þæs wyrmes wig   wide gesyne,
nearofages nið   nean ond feorran,
hu se guðsceaða   Geata leode
hatode ond hynde;   hord eft gesceat,
dryhtsele dyrnne   ær dæges hwile.
Hæfde landwara   lige befangen,
bæle ond bronde;   beorges getruwode,
wiges ond wealles;   him seo wen geleah.
Þa wæs Biowulfe   broga gecyðed
snude to soðe,   þæt his sylfes h[a]m,
bolda selest   brynewylmum mealt,
gifstol Geata.   Þæt ðam godan wæs
hreow on hreðre,   hygesorga mæst;
wende se wisa   þæt he Wealdende
ofer ealde riht,   ecean Dryhtne,
bitre gebulge;   breost innan weoll
þeostrum geþoncum,   swa him geþywe ne wæs.
Hæfde ligdraca   leoda fæsten,
ealond utan,   eorðweard ðone
gledum forgrunden;   him ðæs guðkyning,

close to the dragon's head with stealthy skill.
Thus may a man not fated to die, whom
the favour of the Ruler protects, easily survive
misery and exile. The hoard guardian searched
eagerly along the ground; wanted to find the man
who had acted grievously towards him as he slept.
Hot and fierce-hearted, | often he went round [f.184r]
the barrow on the outside —there was no one there
in that wilderness; yet he rejoiced at warfare,
battle-deeds. At times he turned into the barrow,
searched for the costly cup; he soon discovered
that a man had tampered with the gold,
his rich treasure. The hoard-guardian waited
restless, until evening came;
then was the barrow-guardian enraged,
the hateful foe wished to pay back with flame (for the theft of)
the precious drinking-vessel. Then day departed,
as the serpent wished; no longer would he wait
on the wall, but he went forth with flame,
ready with fire. The beginning was terrifying
for the people in the land, even as it swiftly
ended grievously for their treasure-giver.

XXXIII Then the creature began to belch flames,
burn the bright dwellings; the glow of fire shone,
a terror to men; nothing alive | [f.184v]
would the hateful air-flier leave there.
The serpent's onslaught was widely seen,
his cruelly hostile malice from near and afar,
how the warlike ravager hated and humiliated
the people of the Geats; he hastened back to the hoard,
to his secret splendid hall, ere it was day.
He had encircled the land-dwellers with flame,
with fire and burning; he trusted in the barrow,
his fighting power and wall, his hope deceived him.
Then was the terror made known to Beowulf,
truly quickly, that his own home,
best of buildings, had melted in surges of fire,
the gift-seat of the Geats. That was sorrow
to the good man's heart, greatest of griefs;
the wise man thought that, breaking
established law, he had sorely offended
the Ruler, eternal Lord; within his breast welled up
dark thoughts, as was not his wont.
The fire-dragon had destroyed with flames
the people's stronghold, the coastal land,
the earth-guard; for that the war-king,

Wedera þioden, wræce leornode.
Heht him þa gewyrcean wigendra hleo
eallirenne, eorla dryhten,
wigbord wrætlic; | wisse he gearwe [f.185r]
þæt him holtwudu he[lpan] ne meahte,
lind wið lige. Sceolde [læn]daga
æþeling ærgod ende gebidan,
worulde lifes, ond se wyrm somod,
þeah ðe hordwelan heolde lange.
Oferhogode ða hringa fengel
þæt he þone widflogan weorode gesohte,
sidan herge; no he him þ[a] sæcce ondred,
ne him þæs wyrmes wig for wiht dyde,
eafoð ond ellen, forðon he ær fela,
nearo neðende, niða gedigde,
hildehlemma, syðan he Hroðgares,
sigoreadig secg, sele fælsode,
ond æt guðe forgrap Grendeles mægum
laðan cynnes.
                No þæt læsest wæs
hondgemot[a] þær mon Hygelac sloh,
syððan Geata cyning guðe ræsum,
freawine folca Freslondum on,
Hreðles eafora hiorodryncum swealt,
bille gebeaten. Þonan Biowulf com
sylfes cræfte, sundnytte dreah;
hæfde him on earme | [eorla] þritigra [f.185v]
hildegeatwa þa he to holme [st]ag.
Nealles Hetware hremge þorf[t]on
feðewiges, þe him foran ongean
linde bæron; lyt eft becwom
fram þam hildfrecan hames niosan.
Oferswam ða sioleða bigong sunu Ecgðeowes,
earm anhaga eft to leodum,
þær him Hygd gebead hord ond rice,
beagas ond bregostol; bearne ne truwode,
þæt he wið ælfylcum eþelstolas
healdan cuðe, ða wæs Hygelac dead.
No ðy ær feasceafte findan meahton
æt ðam æðelinge ænige ðinga
þæt he Heardrede hlaford wære,
oððe þone cynedom ciosan wolde;
hwæðre he hi[ne] on folce freondlarum heold,
estum mid are, oððæt he yldra wearð,
Weder-Geatum weold.
                Hyne wræcmæcgas

the prince of the Weders, planned vengeance on him.
Then the protector of warriors, the lord of eorls,
ordered a wondrous shield,
all of iron, to be made; | he knew well [f.185r]
that forest-wood could not help him,
linden shield against fire. The prince of proven excellence
was come to the end of his transitory days —
of life in the the world — and the serpent also,
though he had held long his hoarded wealth.
Then the prince of rings disdained
to seek out the far-flier with a host of men,
a large army; he feared not the fight,
nor did he think much of the serpent's fighting power,
strength and courage, because he, risking harsh straits
had previously survived many combats
and the crash of battles, after he had cleansed
Hrothgar's hall, victorious warrior,
and crushed in combat Grendel's kin,
of loathsome race.
Nor was that the least
of hand-to-hand encounters in which Hygelac was slain,
when the king of the Geats in the onslaught of battle,
noble lord and friend of the people, the son of Hrethel,
in Friesland died of sword-drinks,
struck by the sword. Beowulf came thence
by his own strength, performed a feat of swimming;
he carried on his arm the battle-gear
of thirty eorls, when towards the sea he | went. [f.185v]
The Hetware had no cause to boast
of the battle on foot, when against him
they bore linden shields; few escaped
from that warrior to go back to their home.
Then the son of Ecgtheow swam across the sea's expanse
back to his people, a wretched solitary wanderer,
where Hygd offered him wealth and a kingdom,
rings and a royal throne; she trusted not
that her son could hold his ancestral throne
against hostile hosts, now Hygelac was dead.
Yet those destitute people could not in any way
prevail upon the prince
to be Heardred's lord,
or to accept the royal power;
yet he supported him among the people by friendly counsel,
kindly with honour, until he grew older,
ruled the Weder-Geats.
Exiles, the sons of Ohthere,

ofer sæ sohtan, suna Ohteres;
hæfdon hy forhealden helm Scylfinga,
þone selestan sæcyninga
þara ðe in Swiorice sinc brytnade,
mærne | þeoden. Him þæt to mearce wearð; [f.186r]
he þær [f]or feorme feorhwunde hleat,
sweordes swengum, sunu Hygelaces;
ond him eft gewat Ongenðiowes bearn
hames niosan syððan Heardred læg,
let ðone bregostol Biowulf healdan,
Geatum wealdan; þæt wæs god cyning.
XXXIIII Se ðæs leodhryres lean gemunde
uferan dogrum: Eadgilse wearð
feasceaftum freond, folc gestepte
ofer sæ side sunu Ohteres,
wigum ond wæpnum; he gewræc syððan
cealdum cearsiðum, cyning ealdre bineat.
Swa he niða gehwane genesen hæfde,
sliðra geslyhta, sunu Ecgðiowes,
ellenweorca, oð ðone anne dæg,
þe he wið þam wyrme gewegan sceolde.
Gewat þa twelfa sum torne gebolgen
dryhten Geata dracan sceawian;
hæfde þa gefrunen hwanan sio fæhð aras,
bealonið biorna; him to bearme | cwom [f.186v]
maðþumfæt mære þurh ðæs meldan hond.
Se wæs on ðam ðreate þreotteoða secg
se ðæs orleges or onstealde;
hæft hygegiomor sceolde hean ðonon
wong wisian. He ofer willan giong
to ðæs ðe he eorðsele anne wisse,
hlæw under hrusan holmwylme neh,
yðgewinne; se wæs innan full
wrætta ond wira. Weard unhiore,
gearo guðfreca goldmaðmas heold
eald under eorðan; næs þæt yðe ceap
to gegangenne gumena ænigum.
Gesæt ða on næsse niðheard cyning
þenden hælo abead heorðgeneatum,
goldwine Geata. Him wæs geomor sefa,
wæfre ond wælfus, wyrd ungemete neah,
se ðone gomelan gretan sceolde,
secean sawle hord, sundur gedælan
lif wið lice; no þon lange wæs
feorh æþelinges flæsce bewunden.
Biowulf maþelade, bearn Ecgðeowes:

sought him over the sea;
they had rebelled against the protector of the Scylfings,
the best of the sea-kings
who in Sweden distributed treasure,
a famous | prince. That was his life's end; [f.186r]
he, son of Hygelac, in return for his hospitality,
received a mortal wound from sword-strokes,
and the son of Ongentheow went back again
to seek his home when Heardred was laid low;
he let Beowulf occupy the throne,
rule over the Geats; that was a good king.

XXXIIII In later days he kept in mind retribution
for the prince's fall: he became a friend
of the destitute Eadgils, with a troop he supported
the son of Ohthere over the wide sea,
with warriors and weapons; he took vengeance afterwards
by bitter forays bringing grief; he deprived the king of life.
Thus had the son of Ecgtheow survived
each combat, fierce battle,
courageous deed, until the day
on which he had to do battle with the serpent.
Then, one of twelve, the lord of the Geats went,
raging with anger, to look upon the dragon;
he had learned then whence the feud arose,
dire affliction to men; into his possession had | come [f.186v]
the famous precious vessel through the hand of the informer.
He was the thirteenth man in that company
who had brought about the beginning of that strife,
a sad-hearted slave —abject thence, he had to show
the place. Against his wish he went
to where he he knew of an earth-hall,
a barrow under ground near the surging sea,
the tossing waves; within, it was full
of ornate objects and filigrees. The monstrous keeper,
the ready warrior, guarded golden treasures,
grown old beneath the earth; that was no easy bargain
for any man to obtain.
Then the king, hardy in conflict, sat down on the headland,
wished his hearth-companions good luck,
the gold-giving friend of the Geats. His heart was sad,
restless and ready for death, exceedingly close was the fate
that would come upon the old man,
seek out his soul's hoard, part asunder
life from body; not for long after that was
the prince's life enclosed in flesh.
Beowulf spoke, son of Ecgtheow:

'Fela ic on giogoðe   guðræsa genæs,
orleghwila;   ic þæt eall gemon. | [f.187r]
Ic wæs syfanwintre   þa mec sinca baldor,
freawine folca   æt minum fæder genam;
heold mec ond hæfde   Hreðel cyning,
geaf me sinc ond symbel,   sibbe gemunde;
næs ic him to life   laðra owihte,
beorn in burgum   þonne his bearna hwylc,
Herebeald ond Hæðcyn   oððe Hygelac min.
Wæs þam yldestan   ungedefelice
mæges dædum   morþorbed stred,
syððan hyne Hæðcyn   of hornbogan,
his freawine   flane geswencte,
miste mercelses   ond his mæg ofscet,
broðor oðerne   blodigan gare.
Þæt wæs feohleas gefeoht,   fyrenum gesyngad,
hreðre hygemeðe;   sceolde hwæðre swa þeah
æðeling unwrecen   ealdres linnan.
   Swa bið geomorlic   gomelum ceorle
to gebidanne,   þæt his byre ride
giong on galgan;   þonne he gyd wrece,
sarigne sang,   þonne his sunu hangað
hrefne to hroðre,   ond he him help[e] ne mæg,
eald ond infrod,   ænige gefremman.
Symble bið gemyndgad   morna gehwylce |
eaforan ellorsið;   oðres ne gymeð   [f.187v]
to gebidanne   burgum in innan
yrfeweardas,   þonne se an hafað
þurh deaðes nyd   dæda gefondad.
Gesyhð sorhcearig   on his suna bure,
winsele westne,   windge reste
reote berofene;   ridend swefað,
hæleð in hoðman;   nis þær hearpan sweg,
gomen in geardum,   swylce ðær iu wæron.
XXXV Gewiteð þonne on sealman,   sorhleoð gæleð
an æfter anum;   þuhte him eall to rum,
wongas ond wicstede.
                                   Swa Wedra helm
æfter Herebealde   heortan sorge
weallinde wæge;   wihte ne meahte
on ðam feorhbonan   fæghðe gebetan;
no ðy ær he þone heaðorinc   hatian ne meahte
laðum dædum,   þeah him leof ne wæs.
He ða mid þære sorhge   þe him [t]o sar belamp
gumdream ofgeaf,   Godes leoht geceas;
eaferum læfde,   swa deð eadig mon,

'In youth I survived many rushes of battle,
times of war; I remember it all. | [f.187r]
I was seven years of age when the lord of treasures,
lord and friend of peoples, received me from my father;
King Hrethel took charge of me and kept me,
gave me treasure and feasting, kept in mind our kinship;
in his lifetime I was not at all more hateful to him,
as a warrior in the stronghold than any one of his sons,
Herebeald and Hæthcyn or my own Hygelac.
For the eldest a violent death-bed was unfittingly
spread through the deed of a kinsman,
when with an arrow from his horn-bow,
Hæthcyn struck down his lord and friend,
missed the mark and shot dead his kinsman,
one brother the other, with his bloody shaft.
That was a conflict, unatoned for by money,
a grievously wrongful act, wearying to the heart;
yet the ætheling had to lose his life unavenged.
So it is sad for an old ceorl
to endure, that his son should swing
young on the gallows; then he utters a dirge,
a mournful song, when his son hangs,
as a sport for the raven, and he,
very aged and wise, can accomplish nothing.
He is always reminded, each morn,
of his | son's death; he cares not [f.187v]
to wait in his stronghold for a second heir,
when the one, through death's compulsion,
has experienced the last of his deeds.
Sorrowful he looks on his son's dwelling,
the deserted wine-hall, a resting-place of winds,
deprived of joy; the horsemen sleep,
warriors in their graves; there is no sound of harp,
no joy in the dwelling, as there once was.
XXXV So he goes to his bed, chants one song of grief
after another; all too spacious seemed his fields
and dwelling-place.
Thus did the protector of the Weders
bear welling grief in his heart
for Herebeald; not at all could
he avenge that violent deed on the slayer;
none the sooner could he show hatred for the warrior
with hostile deeds, though he was not dear to him.
Then with the bitter grief that befell him
he gave up human joy, chose God's light;
to his sons he left, as a prosperous man does,

lond ond leodbyrig   þa he of life gewat.
  Þa | wæs synn ond sacu   Sweona ond Geata   [f.188r]
ofer [w]id wæter,   wroht gemæne,
herenið hearda,   syððan Hreðel swealt,
oððe him Ongenðeowes   eaferan wæran
frome fyrdhwate,   freode ne woldon
ofer heafo healdan,   ac ymb Hreosnabeorh
eatolne inwitscear   oft gefremedon.
Þæt mægwine   mine gewræcan,
fæhðe ond fyrene,   swa hyt gefræge wæs,
þeah ðe oðer his   ealdre gebohte,
heardan ceape;   Hæðcynne wearð,
Geata dryhtne,   guð onsæge.
Þa ic on morgne gefrægn   mæg oðerne
billes ecgum   on bonan stælan,
þær Ongenþeow   Eofores niosað;
guðhelm toglad,   gomela Scylfing
hreas [hilde]blac;   hond gemunde
fæhðo genoge,   feorhsweng ne ofteah.
  Ic him þa maðmas   þe he me sealde
geald æt guðe,   swa me gifeðe wæs,
leohtan sweorde;   he me lond forgeaf,
eard eðelwyn.   Næs him ænig þearf
þæt he to Gifðum   oððe to Gar-Denum
oððe in Swiorice   secean þurfe | [f.188v]
wyrsan wigfrecan,   weorðe gecypan;
symle ic him on feðan   beforan wolde,
ana on orde,   ond swa to aldre sceall
sæcce fremman   þenden his sweord þolað
þæt mec ær ond sið   oft gelæste,
syððan ic for dugeðum   Dæghrefne wearð
to handbonan,   Huga cempan.
Nalles he ða frætwe   Frescyning[e],
breostweorðunge   bringan moste,
ac in c[a]mp[e] gecrong   cumbles hyrde,
æþeling on elne;   ne wæs ecg bona,
ac him hildegrap   heortan wylmas,
banhus gebræc.   Nu sceall billes ecg,
hond ond heard sweord   ymb hord wigan.'
  Beowulf maðelode,   beotwordum spræc
niehstan siðe: 'Ic geneðde fela
guða on geogoðe;   gyt ic wylle,
frod folces weard,   fæhðe secan,
mærð[u] fremman,   gif mec se mansceaða
of eorðsele   ut geseceð.'
Gegrette ða   gumena gehwylcne,

land and towns, when he departed from life.
Then | was there enmity and strife between Swedes and Geats,
a mutual feud over the wide water, [f.188r]
warlike enmity, after Hrethel died,
and the sons of Ongentheow were
bold and active in war, would keep no friendship
over the seas, but around Hreosnabeorh
often carried out malicious killing.
That did my dear kinsmen avenge,
the feud and the crime, as was well known,
though one of them paid for it with his life,
a hard bargain; to Hæthcyn,
lord of the Geats, the war was fatal.
I have heard that in the morning one kinsman
with sword's edge then took vengeance for the other
on his slayer, when Ongentheow attacked Eofor;
the war-helmet split, the old Scylfing
fell pale from battle; his hand remembered
many feuds, it held not back the deadly blow.
With my gleaming sword I repaid in battle
as was granted me by fate, the treasures
he bestowed on me; he gave me land,
an ancestral seat. For him there was no need
that, among the Gifthas, or the Spear-Danes,
or in Sweden, he should have to seek
to buy with treasure an | inferior warrior; [f.188v]
I would always go before him in the foot-troop,
alone in the vanguard, and so throughout my life
shall I do battle, while this sword endures
that has often been of service to me,
early and late, ever since I was Dæghrefn's
slayer before the warrior host, champion of the Hugas.
Not at all could he fetch the Frisian king
the adornments, the breast-ornament;
but he, the standard-keeper, fell in battle,
an ætheling in valour; nor was sword's edge the slayer,
but my hostile grasp crushed the surges of his heart,
his bone-house. Now shall sword's edge,
hand and hard blade, do battle for the hoard.'
Beowulf spoke, uttered words in boast
for the last time: 'I ventured upon many
battles in my youth; still will I,
old guardian of the people, seek out conflict,
accomplish a glorious deed, if the wicked ravager
will come to me outside his earthen hall.'
Then he greeted each of the men,

hwate helmberend   hindeman siðe,
swæse gesiðas: 'Nolde ic sweord beran,
wæpen to wyrme, | gif ic wiste hu [f.189r]
wið ðam aglæcean   elles meahte
gylpe wiðgripan,   swa ic gio wið Grendle dyde;
ac ic ðær heaðufyres   hates wene,
[o]reðes ond [a]ttres;   forðon ic me on hafu
bord ond byrnan.   Nelle ic beorges weard
oferfleon fotes trem,   ac unc [furður] sceal
weorðan æt wealle   swa unc wyrd geteoð
Metod manna gehwæs.   Ic eom on mode from
þæt ic wið þone guðflogan   gylp ofersitte.
Gebide ge on beorge   byrnum werede,
secgas on searwum,   hwæðer sel mæge
æfter wælræse   wunde gedygan
uncer twega.   Nis þæt eower sið,
ne gemet mannes   nef[ne] min anes,
[þæ]t he wið aglæcean   eofoðo dæle,
eorlscype efne.   Ic mid elne sceall
gold gegangan,   oððe guð nimeð,
feorhbealu frecne   frean eowerne!'
  Aras ða bi ronde   rof oretta,
heard under helme,   hiorosercean bær
under stancleofu,   strengo getruwode
anes mannes.   Ne bið swylc earges sið!
Geseah ða be wealle | se ðe worna fela [f.189v]
gumcystum god   guða gedigde,
hildehlemma,   þonne hnitan feðan,
sto[n]dan stanbogan,   stream ut þonan
brecan of beorge;   wæs þære burnan wælm
heaðofyrum hat;   ne meahte horde neah
unbyrnende   ænige hwile
deop gedygan   for dracan lege.
Let ða of breostum,   ða he gebolgen wæs,
Weder-Geata leod   word ut faran,
stearcheort styrmde;   stefn in becom
heaðotorht hlynnan   under harne stan.
Hete wæs onhrered,   hordweard oncniow
mannes reorde;   næs ðær mara fyrst
freode to friclan.   From ærest cwom
oruð aglæcean   ut of stane,
hat hildeswat;   hruse dynede.
Biorn under beorge   bordrand onswaf
wið ðam gryregieste,   Geata dryhten;
ða wæs hringbogan   heorte gefysed
sæcce to seceanne.   Sweord ær gebræd

bold warriors in helmets, his dear companions,
for the last time: 'I would not bear a sword,
a weapon against the serpent, | if I knew how else [f.189r]
I could come to grips with the fierce assailant
in accordance my pledge, as erst I did with Grendel;
but there I expect deadly hot fire,
breath and venom; therefore, I have on me
shield and byrny. From the barrow-guardian
I will not flee a foot's step, but at the wall
it shall be as the Creator of every man
allots our destiny to us. I am bold at heart so that I may
forbear from making a vow against the flying enemy.
Wait on the barrow, ye warriors in arms,
protected by byrnies, to see which of us two
may better survive wounds,
after the deadly onslaught. It is not your exploit,
nor is it fitting for any man save me alone,
that he spend his strength against the fierce assailant,
perform heroic deeds. By my valour will I
win gold; or war, terrible deadly harm,
will take your lord!'
Then the brave warrior arose with his shield,
bold beneath his helmet, bore his battle-shirt
beneath the rocky cliffs, trusted the strength
of one man. Such is no cowardly course of action!
Then he saw by the wall | —he, who, [f.189v]
excellent in virtues, had survived many
crashes of battle, when foot-troops clashed—
a stone arch standing, whence burst a stream
out of the barrow; that surging stream
was hot with deadly fire; near the hoard
he could not any while survive without burning
because of the dragon's flames in the depths.
When he was enraged, the man of the Weder-Geats
allowed a cry to break from his breast,
strong-hearted, shouted; his voice clear in battle
went in reverberating, under the grey stone.
Hatred was aroused — the guardian of the hoard
recognized the man's speech; there was no more time
to ask for friendship. First came from out
the stone the fierce monster's breath,
hot battle-sweat; the ground resounded.
The warrior below the barrow, lord of the Geats,
swung his shield-rim against the dreadful stranger;
then was the coiled creature's heart incited
to seek battle. The good war-king

god guðcyning, gomele lafe,
ecgum un[s]law; æghwæðrum wæs
bealohycgendra | broga fram oðrum. [f.190r]
Stiðmod gestod wi[ð] steapne rond
winia bealdor, ða se wyrm gebeah
snude tosomne; he on searwum bad.
Gewat ða byrnende gebogen scriðan,
to gescipe scyndan. Scyld wel gebearg
life ond lice læssan hwile
mærum þeodne þonne his myne sohte,
ðær he þy fyrste forman dogore
wealdan moste, swa him wyrd ne gescraf
hreð æt hilde. Hond up abræd
Geata dryhten, gryrefahne sloh
incgelafe, þæt sio ecg gewac
brun on bane, bat unswiðor
þonne his ðiodcyning þearfe hæfde,
bysigum gebæded. Þa wæs beorges weard
æfter heaðuswenge on hreoum mode,
wearp wælfyre; wide sprungon
hildeleoman. Hreðsigora ne gealp
goldwine Geata; guðbill geswac
nacod æt niðe, swa hyt no sceolde,
iren ærgod. Ne wæs þæt eðe sið,
þæt se mæra maga Ecgðeowes
grundwong þone ofgyfan wolde;
sceolde [ofer] willan wic eardian
elles hwergen, swa | sceal æghwylc mon [f.190v]

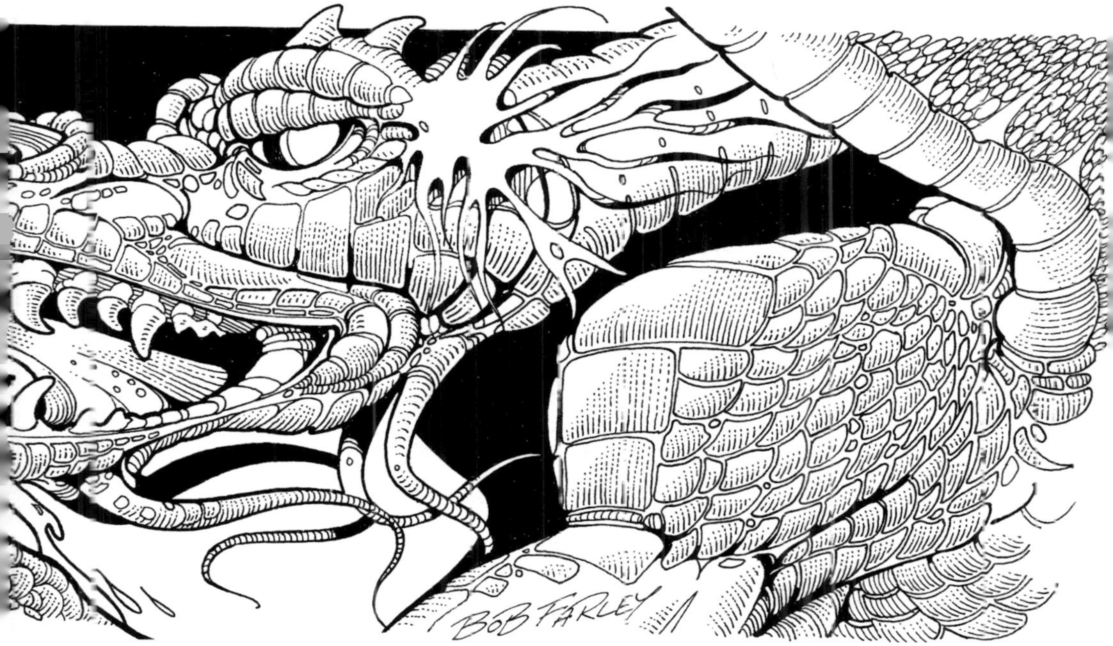

had drawn his sword, an ancient heirloom,
sharp of edge; each of them,
intent upon destruction, | felt horror at the other. [f.190r]
Resolute, with towering shield, stood
the lord of friends, while the serpent coiled itself
swiftly together; he waited in his war-gear.
Then, burning and coiled, it came gliding out —
hastening to its fate. The shield guarded
life and limb well for the famous prince,
but a shorter while than his purpose required,
if on that occasion he were for the first time
to be permitted to prevail, without fate having decreed
triumph for him in battle. The lord of the Geats
swung his hand upwards, struck the patterned horror,
with his mighty heirloom, so that the bright blade
failed on the bone, bit less strongly
than the people's king had need of it,
oppressed by affliction. Then was the barrow's guardian
fierce in spirit, after the battle-stroke,
and spewed deadly fire; far leaped
the battle-light. The gold-giving friend of the Geats
boasted no glorious victories; the naked war-sword,
the hitherto excellent brand, had failed in battle,
as it should not have done. That was no easy journey
for the famous son of Ecgtheow
to give up the earth;
against his wish to have to inhabit
a dwelling-place elsewhere; thus | must each man [f.190v]

alætan lændagas.
Næs ða long to ðon,
þæt ða aglæcean hy eft gemetton.
Hyrte hyne hordweard —hreðer æðme weoll—
niwan stefne; nearo ðrowode,
fyre befongen, se ðe ær folce weold.
Nealles him on heape h[a]ndgesteallan,
æðelinga bearn ymbe gestodon
hildecystum, ac hy on holt bugon,
ealdre burgan. Hiora in anum weoll
sefa wið sorgum; sibb' æfre ne mæg
wiht onwendan þam ðe wel þenceð.
XXXVI Wiglaf wæs haten, Weoxstanes sunu,
leoflic lindwiga, leod Scylfinga,
mæg Ælfheres; geseah his mondryhten
under heregriman hat þrowian.
Gemunde ða ða are, ðe he him ær forgeaf,
wicstede weligne Wægmundinga,
folcrihta gehwylc, swa his fæder ahte.
Ne mihte ða forhabban, hond rond gefeng,
geolwe linde, gomel swyrd geteah;
þæt wæs mid eldum Eanmundes laf, |
suna Ohtere[s]; þam æt sæcce wearð, [f.191r]
wræcca[n] wineleasum Weohsta[n] bana
meces ecgum, ond his magum ætbær
brunfagne helm, hringde byrnan,
ealdsweord etonisc. Þæt him Onela forgeaf,
his gædelinges guðgewædu,
fyrdsearo fuslic; no ymbe ða fæhðe spræc,
þeah ðe he his broðor bearn abredwade.
He frætwe geheold fela missera,
bill ond byrnan, oððæt his byre mihte
eorlscipe efnan swa his ærfæder;
geaf him ða mid Geatum guðgewæda
æghwæs unrim þa he of ealdre gewat,
frod on forðweg. Þa wæs forma sið
geongan cempan, þæt he guðe ræs
mid his freodryhtne fremman sceolde.
Ne gemealt him se modsefa, ne his mæg[es] laf
gewac æt wige; þ[æt] se wyrm onfand,
syððan hie togædre gegan hæfdon.
Wiglaf maðelode, wordrihta fela
sægde gesiðum —him wæs sefa geomor—:
'Ic ðæt | mæl geman, þær we medu þegun, [f.188v]
þonne we geheton ussum hlaforde
in biorsele, ðe us ðas beagas geaf,

leave transitory days.
Not long was it until
the fierce warriors closed on each other again.
The hoard's guardian took heart —his breast heaved
with breathing— once again; he who formerly ruled a people
suffered harsh straits, enveloped by flames.
Not at all did his comrades, in a band,
sons of æthelings, stand around him
with martial virtue; but they fled to the wood,
saved their lives. In one of them the heart
surged with sorrows; nothing can ever
turn aside kinship for one who thinks rightly.

XXXVI He was called Wiglaf, son of Weohstan,
a beloved shield-warrior, a man of the Scylfings,
kinsman of Ælfhere; he saw his liege lord
suffer the heat beneath his helmet.
Then he remembered the property, which formerly he granted him,
the rich dwelling-place of the Wægmundings,
each folk-right, as his father had possessed.
He could not then restrain himself; his hand grasped the shield,
the yellow linden-wood, drew the ancient sword;
it was among men the heirloom of Eanmund, | [f.191r]
son of Ohthere; Weohstan slew
the friendless exile in battle,
with sword's edge, and carried away to his kinsmen
the bright helmet, the ringed byrny,
the old giant-wrought sword. Onela gave him that,
his kinsman's war garments,
ready war-gear; he spoke not about the feud,
though he had slain his brother's son.
He kept the adornments many half-years,
sword and byrny, until his son could
perform doughty deeds, like his late father;
then among the Geats he gave a countless number
of war garments of every kind, when he departed,
old, on his way forth. That was the first time
the young warrior was to perform
in the battle-onslaught with his noble lord.
His spirit did not weaken, nor did his kinsman's
heirloom fail in the fight; the serpent discovered that,
when they had come together.
Wiglaf spoke, uttered many fitting words,
said to his comrades —sad was his heart—:
'I remember that time when we drank mead, [f.191v]
when in the beer-hall we promised
our lord, who gave us these rings,

þæt we him ða guðgetawa   gyldan woldon
gif him þyslicu   þearf gelumpe,
helmas ond heard sweord.   Ðe he usic on herge geceas
to ðyssum siðfate   sylfes willum,
onmunde usic mærða,   ond me þas maðmas geaf,
þe he usic garwigend   gode tealde,
hwate helmberend   —þeah ðe hlaford us
þis ellenweorc   ana aðohte
to gefremmanne,   folces hyrde,
forðam he manna mæst   mærða gefremede,
dæda dollicra.   Nu is se dæg cumen
þæt ure mandryhten   mægenes behofað
godra guðrinca.   Wutun gongan to,
helpan hildfruman   þenden hyt sy,
gledegesa grim.   God wat on mec
þæt me is micle leofre   þæt minne lichaman
mid minne goldgyfan   gled fæðmie.
Ne þynceð me gerysne   þæt we rondas beren
eft to earde   nemne we æror mægen
fane gefyllan, | feorh ealgian [f.192r]
Wedra ðeodnes.   Ic wat geare
þæt næron ealdgewyrht   þæt he ana scyle
Geata duguðe   gnorn þrowian,
gesigan æt sæcce;   urum sceal sweord ond helm,
byrne ond b[ea]duscrud   bam gemæne.'
Wod þa þurh þone wælrec,   wigheafolan bær
frean on fultum,   fea worda cwæð:
'Leofa Biowulf,   læst eall tela,
swa ðu on geoguðfeore   geara gecwæde
þæt ðu ne alæte   be ðe lifigendum
dom gedreosan;   scealt nu dædum rof,
æðeling anhydig,   ealle mægene
feorh ealgian;   ic ðe fullæstu.'
Æfter ðam wordum   wyrm yrre cwom,
atol inwitgæst   oðre siðe
fyrwylmum fah   fionda nios[i]an,
laðra manna.   Lig yðum for,
born bord wið rond;   byrne ne meahte
geongum garwigan   geoce gefremman,
ac se maga geonga   under his mæges scyld
elne geeode,   þa his agen [wæs]
gledum forgrunden.   Þa gen guðcyning
m[ærða] gemunde,   mægenstrengo sloh
hildebille,   þæt hyt on heafolan stod
niþe genyded;   Nægling forbærst,
geswac æt sæcce   sweord Biowulfes, |

that we would repay him for the war-gear,
if a need such as this befell him,
helmets and sharp swords. For this reason he chose us
of his own will among the host for this venture,
thought us worthy of glory, and gave me these treasures,
because he reckoned us good spear-fighters,
valiant warriors in helmets —though our lord,
protector of the people, intended to accomplish
this courageous deed unaided,
because he among men accomplished the most feats of glory,
audacious deeds. Now is the day come
when our liege lord needs the strength
of valiant warriors. Let us go to him,
and help our leader in battle, while the heat,
grim fire-terror, persists. As for me, God knows,
it is much dearer to me that the fire should enfold
my body with my gold-giving lord.
It does not seem fitting to me that we should bear shields
back to our home, unless we can first
kill the foe, | defend the life of the prince [f.192r]
of the Weders. I know well
that, by his past deeds, he does not deserve alone
among the host of Geats to suffer affliction,
fall in battle; both of us must share together
sword and helmet, byrny and battle-shroud.'
Then he went through the deadly reek; bore his helmet
to the aid of his lord, spoke a few words:
'Dear Beowulf, do all things well,
just as thou didst say in thy youth long ago,
that thou wouldst never while alive allow
thy glory to decline; now must thou, resolute ætheling,
mighty in deeds, defend thy life
with all thy strength: I shall help thee.'
After these words, the serpent came angrily
a second time, the terrible malicious creature,
glowing with surging fire, to attack his foes,
the hateful men. Flame advanced in waves,
the shield burned right up to the boss; the byrny
could not provide help to the young spear-warrior,
but the young man under his kinsman's shield
fought valiantly, when his own [was]
destroyed by flames. Then the war-king,
mindful again of glory, with great strength struck
with his battle-sword, so that it stuck in the head,
impelled by hostility; Nægling broke,
Beowulf's sword, | ancient, steel-grey, [f.192v]

gomol ond grægmæl. Him þæt gifeðe ne wæs [f.192v]
þæt him irenna ecge mihton
helpan æt hilde; wæs sio hond to strong,
se ðe meca gehwane mine gefræge,
swenge ofersohte, þonne he to sæcce bær
wæpen wund[r]um heard; næs him wihte ðe sel.
Þa wæs þeodsceaða þriddan siðe,
frecne fyrdraca fæhða gemyndig,
ræsde on ðone rofan þa him rum ageald,
hat ond heaðogrim Heals ealne ymbefeng
biteran banum; he geblodegod wearð
sawuldriore, swat yðum weoll.
XXXVII Ða ic æt þearfe [gefrægn] þeodcyninges
andlongne eorl ellen cyðan,
cræft ond cenðu, swa him gecynde wæs.
Ne hedde he þæs heafolan, ac sio hand gebarn
modiges mannes þær he his mæg[es] healp,
þæt he þone niðgæst nioðor hwene sloh,
secg on searwum, þæt ðæt sweord gedeaf
fah ond fæted, þæt ðæt fyr ongon
sweðrian syððan. Þa gen sylf cyning
geweold his gewitte, wællseaxe gebræd
biter ond beaduscearp þæt he on byrnan wæg;
forwrat Wedra | helm wyrm on middan. [f.193r]
Feond gefyldan —ferh ellen wræc—
ond hi hyne þa begen abroten hæfdon,
sibæðelingas. Swylc sceolde secg wesan,
þegn æt ðearfe. Þæt ðam þeodne wæs
siðas[t] sigehwile sylfes dædum,
worlde geweorces.
Ða sio wund ongon
þe him se eorðdraca ær geworhte
swelan ond swellan; he þæt sona onfand,
þæt him on breostum bealonið[e] weoll
attor on innan. Ða se æþeling giong,
þæt he bi wealle wishycgende
gesæt on sesse; seah on enta geweorc,
hu ða stanbogan stapulum fæste
ece eorðreced innan healde.
Hyne þa mid handa heorodreorigne,
þeoden mærne þegn ungemete till,
winedryhten his wætere gelafede,
hilde sædne, ond his hel[m] onspeon.
Biowulf maþelode —he oðer benne spræc,
wunde wælbleate; wisse he gearwe
þæt he dæghwila gedrogen hæfde,

failed him in the battle. It was not granted him
that the edges of swords might
help in the battle; too strong was the hand which,
as I have heard, over-taxed every sword
with its stroke, when he bore to battle
a weapon hardened with wounds; it availed him not at all.
Then, for the third time, the ravager of the people,
the terrible fire-dragon, intent on hostile deeds,
rushed on the brave man, when occasion favoured him,
hot and battle-fierce. It clasped his whole neck
with sharp tusks; he was made bloody
with life-blood, the gore surged in streams.

XXXVII Then, I have heard that, in the need of the people's king,
the eorl at his side displayed his courage,
his strength and boldness, as was natural to him.
He did not pay heed to the head, but the brave man's hand
was burned when he helped his kinsman,
as the man in armour struck the malicious stranger
a little lower down, so that the sword sank in,
gleaming and gold-plated; and then the fire began
to subside. Then the king himself again
controlled his senses, drew the deadly knife,
biting and battle-sharp, that he carried on his byrny;
the | protector of the Weders cut the serpent through the middle.
They had felled the foe —their valour had driven out its life— [f.193r]
and they, the noble kinsmen, had both
destroyed it. Such should a man be,
a thane in time of need! That was the last of the times
of victory for the prince by his own deeds,
of work in the world.
Then the wound
which erewhile the earth-dragon had inflicted on him
began to burn and swell; he soon found out
that the deadly evil welled up in his breast,
the venom within him. Then the ætheling went,
wise in thought, to where he might sit
on a seat by the wall; looked at the work of giants,
how the age-old earth-dwelling held
within it stone arches, secure on pillars.
Then with his hands the most excellent thane
bathed with water the famous prince,
his friend and lord, blood-stained from battle,
wearied with war, and unfastened his helmet.
Beowulf spoke —despite his wounds,
his mortal wounds, he spoke; he knew
full well that he had used up his time

eorðan wyn[ne]; ða wæs eall sceacen
dogorgerimes, deað ungemete neah:
'Nu ic suna minum syllan wolde
guðgewædu, þær me gifeðe swa
ænig yrfe | weard æfter wurde [f.193v]
lice gelenge. Ic þas leode heold
fiftig wintra; næs se folccyning,
ymbesittendra ænig ðara,
þe mec guðwinum gretan dorste,
egesan ðeon. Ic on earde bad
mælgesceafta, heold min tela,
ne sohte searoniðas, ne me swor fela
aða on unriht. Ic ðæs ealles mæg
feorhbennum seoc gefean habban;
forðam me witan ne ðearf Waldend fira
morðorbealo maga, þonne min sceaceð
lif of lice. Nu ðu lungre geong
hord sceawian under harne stan,
Wiglaf leofa, nu se wyrm ligeð,
swefeð sare wund, since bereafod.
Bio nu on ofoste þæt ic ærwelan,
goldæht ongite, gearo sceawige
swegle searogimmas, þæt ic ðy seft mæge
æfter maððumwelan min alætan
lif ond leodscipe, þone ic longe heold.'
XXXVIII Ða ic snude gefrægn sunu Wihstanes
æfter wordcwydum wundum dryhtne
hyran heaðosiocum, hringnet beran,
brogdne beadusercean u[n]der beorges hrof.
Geseah ða sigehreðig, þa he bi sesse geong,
magoþegn | modig maððumsigla fealo, [f.194r]
gold glitinian grunde getenge,
wundur on wealle, ond þæs wyrmes denn,
ealdes uhtflogan, orcas stondan,
fyrnmanna fatu, feormendlease,
hyrstum behrorene. Þær wæs helm monig
eald ond omig, earmbeaga fela
searwum gesæled. Sinc eaðe mæg,
gold on grund[e] gumcynnes gehwone
oferhigian, hyde se ðe wylle.
Swylce he siomian geseah segn eallgylden
heah ofer horde, hondwundra mæst,
gelocen leoðocræftum; of ðam leom[a] stod,
þæt he þone grundwong ongitan meahte,
wræ[t]e giondwlitan. Næs ðæs wyrmes þær
onsyn ænig, ac hyne ecg fornam.

of earthly joy; then was the number of his days
all passed away, death exceedingly close:
'Now should I have wished to give my son
my war garments, if granted (by fate)
that any | heir, belonging to my body, [f.193v]
should come after me. I ruled this people
fifty winters; there was no nation's king
among those dwelling around,
who dared attack me with allies in war,
threaten me with terrors. In my homeland
I awaited destiny, guarded mine well,
nor sought treacherous quarrels, nor sworn
many oaths wrongfully. In all of this I may
have joy, sick with mortal wounds;
for the Ruler of men has no cause to blame me
for the wicked murder of kinsmen, when
my life passes from my body. Now go swiftly
to examine the hoard under the grey stone,
dear Wiglaf, now that the serpent lies dead,
sleeps in death sorely wounded, deprived of treasure.
Haste now, that I may see the ancient riches,
the store of gold, may eagerly examine
the bright finely worked jewels; so that because
of the wealth of treasure I may the more easily leave
my life and people, which I have long held.'
XXXVIII Then I have heard that, after these spoken words,
the son of Weohstan swiftly obeyed his wounded lord,
wounded in battle, went in his mail-coat,
his woven battle-shirt, beneath the roof of the barrow.
There, triumphant in victory, the brave young thane saw,
as he went by the seat, many a precious jewel, [f.194r]
glittering gold lying on the ground,
wondrous objects on the wall, and the serpent's lair,
the old night-flier's, cups standing,
vessels of men of old, lacking a burnisher,
deprived of their adornments. There was many a helm,
ancient and rusty, many an arm-ring,
skilfully twisted. Treasure,
gold in the earth, may easily overpower
any man, hide it though one may.
Also he saw hanging a standard all of gold
high above the hoard, greatest of marvels,
woven by skill of hand; from this a light shone out,
so that he could see the surface of the floor,
behold the jewels. There was no trace there
of the serpent, for the sword had carried it off.

Ða ic on hlæwe gefrægn hord reafian,
eald enta geweorc anne mannan,
him on bearm hl[a]don bunan ond discas
sylfes dome; segn eac genom,
beacna beorhtost. Bill ær gescod
—ecg wæs iren— ealdhalfordes
þam ðara maðma mundbora wæs
longe hwile, ligegesan wæg
hatne for horde, hioroweallende
middelnihtum, | oðþæt he morðre swealt. [f.194v]
Ar wæs on ofoste, eftsiðes georn,
frætwum gefyrðred; hyne fyrwet bræc,
hwæðer collenferð cwicne gemette
in ðam wongstede Wedra þeoden
ellensiocne, þær he hine ær forlet.
He ða mid þam maðmum mærne þioden,
dryhten sinne driorigne fand
ealdres æt ende; he hine eft ongon
wæteres weorpan, oðþæt wordes ord
breosthord þurhbræc.
[Biorncyning spræc]
gomel on gio[h]ðe —gold sceawode—:
'Ic ðara frætwa Frean ealles ðanc,
Wuldurcyninge wordum secge,
ecum Dryhtne, þe ic her on starie,
þæs ðe ic moste minum leodum
ær swyltdæge swylc gestrynan.
Nu ic on maðma hord mi[n]e bebohte
frode feorhlege, fremmað gena
leoda þearfe; ne mæg ic her leng wesan.
Hatað heaðomære hlæw gewyrcean
beorhtne æfter bæle æt brimes nosan;
se scel to gemyndum minum leodum
heah hlifian on Hronesnæsse,
þæt hit sæliðend syððan hatan
Biowulfes biorh, ða ðe brentingas
ofer | floda genipu feorran drifað.' [f.195r]
Dyde him of healse hring gyldenne
þioden þristhydig, þegne gesealde,
geongum garwigan, goldfahne helm,
beah ond byrnan, het hyne brucan well:
'Þu eart endelaf usses cynnes,
Wægmundinga; ealle wyrd fors[w]eo[p]
mine magas to meotodsceafte,
eorlas on elne; ic him æfter sceal.'
Þæt wæs þam gomelan gingæste word

I have heard that one man then plundered the hoard
in the barrow, the ancient work of giants,
loaded his lap with drinking-vessels and dishes,
of his own choice; he also took the standard,
brightest of banners. The aged lord's sword
—its edge was of iron— had already wounded the creature
which had been the guardian of those treasures
for a long while, brought its fire-terror,
hot because of the hoard, fiercely welling
at midnight | until it died a violent death. [f.194v]
  The messenger made haste, eager to journey back,
urged on by the precious things; anxiety oppressed him
whether, bold in spirit, he would find alive
in the place where erstwhile he left him,
deprived of strength, the prince of the Weders.
Then, with the treasures, he found
the famous prince, his lord, bleeding,
at the end of his life; again he began
to sprinkle him with water, until the sword's point
broke through his heart.
[The warrior-king spoke]
the old man in sorrow —looked on the gold—:
'I utter thanks in words to the Lord of all,
the King of glory, the eternal Lord,
for the precious things which I gaze upon here,
for the fact that I have been permitted to win
for my people such gain ere my day of death.
Now that I have sold my old life
for a hoard of treasures, attend ye still
to the people's needs; no longer may I tarry here.
Bid the men famed in battle raise on the sea's headland
a splendid mound after the funeral pyre;
as a reminder to my people
it shall tower high on Hronesness,
so that seafarers may call it thereafter
Beowulf's barrow, when from afar
they sail their ships over misty seas.' [f.195r]
The bold-minded prince took from his neck
the golden ring, gave to the thane,
the young spear-warrior, gold-adorned helmet,
ring and byrny, bade him use them well.
'Thou art the last remaining of our race,
of the Wægmundings; Fate has swept away
all my kinsmen by decree of destiny,
eorls in their valour; I must follow them.'
That was the last word from the old man's

breostgehygdum ær he bæl cure,
hate heaðowylmas; him of h[re]ðre gewat
sawol secean soðfæstra dom.
[XXXVIIII] Ða wæs gegongen gum[an] unfrodum
earfoðlice, þæt he on eorðan geseah
þone leofestan lifes æt ende
bleate gebæran. Bona swylce læg,
egeslic eorðdraca ealdre bereafod,
bealwe gebæded. Beahhordum leng
wyrm wohbogen wealdan ne moste,
ac hi[ne] irenna ecga fornamon,
hearde heaðoscear[p]e homera lafe,
þæt se widfloga wundum stille
hreas on hrusan hordærne neah.
Nalles | æfter lyfte lacende hwearf [f.195v]
middelnihtum, maðmæhta wlonc
ansyn ywde, ac he eorðan gefeoll
for ðæs hildfruman hondgeweorce.
Huru þæt on lande lyt manna ðah
mægenagendra, mine gefræge,
þeah ðe he dæda gehwæs dyrstig wære,
þæt he wið attorsceaðan oreðe geræsde
oððe hringsele hondum styrede,
gif he wæccende weard onfunde
buon on beorge. Biowulfe wearð
dryhtmaðma dæl deaðe forgolden;
hæfde æghwæð[er] ende gefered
lænan lifes.
Næs ða lang to ðon,
þæt ða hildlatan holt ofgefan,
tydre treowlogan tyne ætsomne,
ða ne dorston ær dareðum lacan
on hyra mandryhtnes miclan þearfe;
ac hy scamiende scyldas bæran,
guðgewædu þær se gomela læg;
wlitan on Wilaf. He gewergad sæt,
feðecempa frean eaxlum neah;
wehte hyne wætre —him wiht ne speo[w].
Ne meahte he on eorðan, ðeah he uðe wel,
on ðam frumgare feorh gehealdan,
ne ðæs Wealdendes wiht oncirran;
wolde dom | Godes dædum rædan [f.192r]
gumena gehwylcum, swa he nu gen deð.
Þa wæs æt ðam geong[an] grim andswaru
eðbegete þam ðe ær his elne forleas.
Wiglaf maðelode, Weohstanes sunu,

thoughts of the heart ere he chose the pyre,
hot hostile flames; his soul departed from his breast
to seek the judgment of righteous men.
[XXXVIIII] Then was it a bitter experience
for the young man, that he saw on the ground
the most beloved of men suffering pitiably
at the end of his life. His slayer also lay
deprived of life, the terrible earth-dragon
overwhelmed by ruin. The coiled serpent
could no longer rule over the ring-hoard,
but iron swords, hard, battle-sharp,
the remnants of hammers, had destroyed it:
so that the wide-flier, fell on the earth,
motionless from its wounds, near its treasure-house.
No more | did it move about, flying through the air [f.195v]
at midnight, exulting in its precious possessions,
displaying itself; but it fell to the earth
through the deed of the war-leader's hand.
Yet, as I have heard, it has profited few
of the mighty men in the land,
though daring in every deed, to make a rush
against the breath of the venomous ravager,
or disturb with hands the hall of rings,
if he discovered the guardian awake
who dwells in the barrow. Beowulf's share
of the noble treasures was paid for with death;
each of the two had reached the end
of transitory life.

It was not long until
the laggards in battle left the wood,
ten cowardly traitors together,
who durst not before with spears
fight in their lord's great need;
but, ashamed, they carried their shields,
their war garments, to where the old man lay;
gazed at Wiglaf. He, the foot-warrior,
exhausted, sat near his lord's shoulders;
revived him with water —not at all did he succeed.
He could not keep his chieftain's life
on earth, though dearly he wished it,
nor change anything ordained by the Ruler;
for the decree of | God would rule [f.196r]
the deeds of each man, just as it still does now.
Then for those who had lost their courage
it was easy to obtain a grim answer from the youth.
Wiglaf spoke, son of Weohstan,

sec[g] sarigferð —seah on unleofe—:
'Þæt, la, mæg secgan se ðe wyle soð specan,
þæt se mondryhten, se eow ða maðmas geaf,
eoredgeatwe, þe ge þær on standað,
—þonne he on ealubence oft gesealde
healsittendum helm ond byrnan,
þeoden his þegnum, swylce he þrydlicost
ower feor oððe neah findan meahte—
þæt he genunga guðgewædu
wraðe forwurpe, ða hyne wig beget.
Nealles folccyning fyrdgesteallum
gylpan þorfte; hwæðre him God uðe,
sigora Waldend, þæt he hyne sylfne gewræc
ana mid ecge, þa him wæs elnes þearf.
Ic him lifwraðe lytle meahte
ætgifan æt guðe, ond ongan swa þeah
ofer min gemet mæges helpan.
Symle wæs þy sæmra, þonne ic sweorde drep
ferhðgeniðlan, fyr unswiðor
weoll of gewitte. [W]ergendra to lyt
þrong ymbe þeoden, þa hyne sio | þrag becwom. [f.196v]
[N]u sceal sincþego ond swyrdgifu,
eall eðelwyn eowrum cynne,
lufen alicgean; londrihtes mot
þære mægburge monna æghwylc
idel hweorfan, syððan æðelingas
feorran gefricgean fleam eowerne,
domleasan dæd. Deað bið sella
eorla gehwylcum þonne edwitlif!'

XL Heht ða þæt heaðoweorc to hagan blodan
up ofer ecgclif, þær þæt eorlweorod
morgenlongne dæg modgiomor sæt,
bordhæbbende, bega on wenum,
endedogores ond eftcymes
leofes monnes. Lyt swigode
niwra spella se ðe næs gerad,
ac he soðlice sægde ofer ealle:
'Nu is wilgeofa Wedra leoda,
dryhten Geata deaðbedde fæst,
wunað wælreste wyrmes dædum;
him on efn ligeð ealdorgewinna
s[e]xbennum seoc; sweorde ne meahte
on ðam aglæcean ænige þinga
wunde gewyrcean. Wiglaf siteð
ofer Biowulfe, byre Wihstanes,
eorl ofer oðrum unlifigendum,

the sad-hearted man —looked on the unloved ones—:
'Anyone who wishes to speak the truth may indeed say
of the liege lord who gave you those treasures,
the war-gear in which you are standing there
—when at the mead-bench he often gave to those
sitting in the hall a helmet and byrny,
as a prince to his thanes, the most splendid
that he could find anywhere, far or near—
that when war came upon him he had utterly
and grievously thrown away those war garments.
The people's king had no cause to boast
of his comrades in arms; yet God,
Ruler of victories, granted that he avenge himself
alone with his sword, when he had need of courage.
Little life-protection was I able to give him
in the combat; and yet I tried to help
my kinsman beyond my power.
The deadly foe was always the weaker,
after I struck it with my sword, fire welled out
less strongly from its head. Too few defenders
pressed forward around the prince, when the time | came. [f.196v]
Now shall receiving of treasure and giving of swords,
all enjoyment of hereditary land,
beloved homeland, cease; each man
of your kindred must wander about,
deprived of his land-right, when æthelings
from afar learn of your flight,
your inglorious deed. Death is better
for all eorls than a life of disgrace!'

XL Then he ordered the battle-deed be announced in the enclosure,
up over the sea-cliff, where the band of warriors
sat all morning long, sad at heart,
shield-bearers, expecting one of two things,
the beloved man's last day
or his return. He who rode up to the headland
held back little of the late tidings,
but he said truly in the hearing of all:
'Now is the joy-giver of the people of the Weders,
the lord of the Geats, fast on his death-bed;
lies on a couch of slaughter by the serpent's deeds;
beside him lies his deadly foe
stricken with dagger-wounds; with his sword he could not
in any way inflict a wound
on the fierce assailant. Wiglaf,
son of Weohstan, sits by Beowulf,
the living eorl by the lifeless one,

healdeð higemæðum | heafodwearde [f.197r]
leofes ond laðes.
Nu ys leodum wen
orleghwile, syððan under[ne]
Froncum ond Frysum fyll cyninges
wide weorðeð. Wæs sio wroht scepen
heard wið Hugas, syððan Higelac cwom
faran flotherge on Fresna land,
þær hyne Hetware hilde ge[n]ægdon,
elne geeodon mid ofermægene,
þæt se byrnwiga bugan sceolde,
feoll on feðan; nalles frætwe geaf
ealdor dugoðe. Us wæs a syððan
Merewioingas milts ungyfeðe.
Ne ic te Sweoðeode sibbe oððe treowe
wihte ne wene, ac wæs wide cuð
þætte Ongenðio ealdre besnyðede
Hæðcen Hreþling wið Hrefnawudu,
þa for onmedlan ærest gesohton
Geata leode Guð-Scilfingas.
Sona him se froda fæder Ohtheres,
eald ond egesfull [o]ndslyht ageaf,
abreot brimwisan, bryd ah[red]de,
gomela[n] iomeowlan golde berofene,
Onelan modor ond Ohtheres;
ond ða folgode feorhgeniðlan
oððæt hi oðeodon earfoðlice
in Hrefnesholt hlafordlease.
Besæt ða sinherge sweorda lafe
wundum werge; | wean oft gehet [f.197v]
earmre teohhe ondlonge niht,
cwæð, he on mergenne meces ecgum
getan wolde, sum[e] on galgtreowu[m]
[fuglum] to gamene. Frofor eft gelamp
sarigmodum somod ærdæge,
syððan hie Hygelaces horn ond byman,
gealdor ongeaton, þa se goda com
leoda dugoðe on last faran.
XLI Wæs sio swatsawðu Sw[e]ona ond Geata,
wælræs weora wide gesyne,
hu ða folc mid him fæhðe towehton.
Gewat him ða se goda mid his gædelingum,
frod felageomor fæsten secean,
eorl Ongenþio ufor oncirde;
hæfde Higelaces hilde gefrunen,
wlonces wigcræft; wiðres ne truwode,

in weariness of mind, keeps watch at the heads | [f.197r]
of friend and foe
Now the people can expect
a time of war, when the king's death
is manifest to Franks and Frisians,
widely known. Harsh strife was created
against the Hugas when Hygelac came journeying
with a ship-borne force to the land of the Frisians,
where the Hetware subdued him in battle,
brought about by their superior strength
so that he, the byrnied warrior, had to yield;
he fell among his foot-troop; that lord gave
no precious things to his retainers. To us ever since
has the favour of the Merovingians been denied.
I do not at all expect peace or good faith
from the Swedish people, for it is widely known
that Ongentheow took the life
of Hæthcyn, Hrethel's son, near Ravenswood
when the people of the Geats in their arrogance
first attacked the War-Scylfings.
Straightway the aged father of Ohthere,
old and terrible, dealt a counter-stroke,
cut down the sea-king, rescued his wife,
an old woman of a former day, deprived of gold,
Onela's mother and Ohthere's;
then he pursued his deadly foes
until with difficulty they escaped,
lordless, into Ravenswood.
With his standing army he besieged the remnant
wound-wearied, | often vowed misery [f.197v]
to the wretched company the entire night;
said, in the morning with the edges of swords
he would destroy them, hang some on gallows
as sport [for birds]. Comfort had come about
to the sad at heart with the first light of day,
when they heard the sound of Hygelac's horn
and trumpet, when the hero came
following in their track with a host of men.
XLI The bloody trail of Swedes and Geats,
the deadly onslaught of men, was widely visible,
how these folk stirred up the feud between them.
Then the valiant one departed with his kinsmen,
the old man very sad, to seek his stronghold,
the eorl Ongentheow turned aside to higher ground;
he had heard of Hygelac's fighting power,
proud battle-craft; he trusted not in resistance,

þæt he sæmannum   onsacan mihte,
heaðoliðendum   hord forstandan,
bearn ond bryde;   beah eft þonan
eald under eorðweall.   Þa wæs æht boden
Sweona leodum,   segn Higelace[s]
freoðowong þone   for[ð] ofereodon,
syððan Hreðlingas   to hagan þrungon.
Þær wearð Ongenðiow   ecgum sweord[a],
blondenfexa   on bid wrecen,
þæt se þeodcyning   ðafian sceolde
Eafores | anne dom.   Hyne yrringa   [f.198r]
Wulf Wonreding   wæpne geræhte,
þæt him for swenge   swat ædrum sprong
forð under fexe.   Næs he forht swa ðeh,
gomela Scilfing,   ac forgeald hraðe
wyrsan wrixle   wælhlem þone,
syððan ðeodcyning   þyder oncirde.
Ne meahte se snella   sunu Wonredes
ealdum ceorle   [o]ndslyht giofan,
ac he him on heafde   helm ær gescer,
þæt he blode fah   bugan sceolde,
feoll on foldan;   næs he fæge þa git,
ac he hyne gewyrpte,   þeah ðe him wund hrine.
Let se hearda   Higelaces þegn
brad[n]e mece,   þa his broðor læg,
ealdsweord eotonisc   entiscne helm
brecan ofer bordweal;   ða gebeah cyning,
folces hyrde,   wæs in feorh dropen.
Ða wæron monige   þe his mæg wriðon,
ricone arærdon,   ða him gerymed wearð
þæt hie wælstowe   wealdan moston.
Þenden reafode   rinc oðerne,
nam on Ongenðio   irenbyrnan,
heard swyrd hilted,   ond his helm somod;
hares hyrste   Higelace bær.
H[e ðam] frætwum feng   ond him fægre gehet
leana [mid] | leodum,   ond gelæst[e] swa;   [f.198v]
geald þone guðræs   Geata dryhten,
Hreðles eafora,   þa he to ham becom,
Iofore ond Wulfe   mid ofermaðmum,
sealde hiora gehwæðrum   hund þusenda
landes ond locenra beaga   —ne ðorfte him ða lean oðwitan
mon on middangearde,   syðða[n] hie ða mærða geslogon
ond ða Iofore forgeaf   angan dohtor,
hamweorðunge,   hyldo to wedde.
   Þæt ys sio fæhðo   ond se feondscipe,

that he could fight off the seamen,
defend hoard, women and children from
the seafaring warriors; thence the old man drew back
behind an earthen rampart. Then was pursuit given
the people of the Swedes, Hygelac's standards
overran the place of refuge,
once the Hrethlings penetrated the enclosure.
There was the grey-haired Ongentheow
brought to bay by the edges of swords,
the people's king compelled to submit
to Eofor's | judgment alone. Wulf, son of Wonred, [f.198r]
struck him furiously with his weapon,
so that the blood from the stroke spurted out of his veins
beneath his hair. But, unafraid still,
the old Scylfing quickly paid back
the deadly blow with worse exchange,
when the people's king turned in that direction.
The brave son of Wonred could not pay back
the blow the old ceorl had given him,
but he had already cut through the helmet on his head,
so that, stained with blood, he had to bow down;
he fell on the earth; he was not fated to die yet,
but he recovered himself, though the wound hurt him.
Then Hygelac's hardy thane caused his broad sword,
the ancient sword forged by giants, to break
the massive helmet, over the protecting shield,
when his brother lay dead; then the king bowed down,
the people's guardian, mortally wounded.
Many there were who bound his kinsman's wounds,
raised him up swiftly, when space was cleared for them,
so that they were able to possess the place of slaughter.
Then one warrior plundered the other,
took from Ongentheow his iron byrny,
his hard-hilted sword and also his helmet;
bore the grey-haired one's accoutrement to Hygelac.
He received those adornments and courteously promised him
rewards | amid the people; and thus did he fulfil it; [f.198v]
the lord of the Geats, the son of Hrethel,
when he came home, repaid the onslaught in battle
with very great treasures to Eofor and Wulf:
he gave to each of them land and linked rings to the value of
a hundred thousand [sceattas] —for those rewards, no man on earth
need reproach him, since they were achieved by fighting
and then to Eofor he gave his only daughter,
as a pledge of his favour, to honour his home.
That is the feud and the enmity,

wælnið wera, ðæs ðe ic [wen] hafo,
þe us seceað to Sweona leoda,
syððan hie gefricgeað frean userne
ealdorleasne, þone ðe ær geheold
wið hettendum hord ond rice,
æfter hæleða hryre, hwate scild[wi]ga[n],
folcred fremede oððe furður gen
eorlscipe efnde. [Nu] is ofost betost,
þæt we þeodcyning þær sceawian,
ond þone gebringan, þe us beagas geaf,
on adfære. Ne scel anes hwæt
meltan mid þam modigan, ac þær is maðma hord,
gold unrime grimme gecea[po]d,
ond nu æt siðestan sylfes feore
beagas [geboh]te; þa sceall brond fretan,
æled þeccean | —nalles eorl wegan [f.199r]
maððum to gemyndum, ne mægð scyne
habban on healse hringweorðunge,
ac sceal geomormod, golde bereafod,
oft nalles æne elland tredan,
nu se herewisa hleahtor alegde,
gamen ond gleodream. Forðon sceall gar wesan
monig morgenceald mundum bewunden,
hæfen on handa, nalles hearpan sweg
wigend weccean, ac se wonna hrefn
fus ofer fægum fela reordian,
earne secgan, hu him æte speow
þenden he wið wulf wæl reafode.'
Swa se secg hwata secggende wæs
laðra spella; he ne leag fela
wyrda ne worda. Weorod eall aras;
eodon unbliðe under Earnanæs,
wollenteare wundur sceawian.
Fundon ða on sande sawulleasne
hlimbed healdan þone þe him hringas geaf
ærran mælum; þa wæs endedæg
godum gegongen, þæt se guðcyning,
Wedra þeoden wundordeaðe swealt.
Ær hi þær gesegan syllicran wiht,
wyrm on wonge wiðerræhtes þær
laðne licgean; wæs se legdraca
grimlic gry[refah] | gledum beswæled; [f.199v]
se wæs fiftiges fotgemearces
lang on legere; lyftwynne heold
nihtes hwilum, nyðer eft gewat
dennes niosian; wæs ða deaðe fæst,

the deadly hostility of men, as I expect,
for which the people of the Swedes will attack us,
when they learn that our lord
is lifeless, he who formerly protected
hoard and kingdom against enemies,
after the fall of heroes, valiant shield-warriors,
for the benefit of the people and further still
carried out heroic deeds. Now is haste best,
that we may look at the people's king there
and bring him, who gave us rings,
on his way to the funeral pyre. Not just a single share shall melt
away with the brave man, for there is a hoard of treasures,
countless gold, grimly purchased;
and now in the end rings bought
with his own life; these must the fire consume,
the flame enfold — | no eorl shall wear [f.199r]
a jewel in remembrance, nor beautiful woman
have a ring-adornment round her neck,
but, sad at heart, stripped of gold,
they shall tread an alien land, not once but often,
now that the leader of armies has laid aside laughter,
joy and merriment. Therefore shall many a spear,
cold in the morning, be grasped with fingers,
raised aloft with hands; no sound of harp
shall awaken warriors, but the black raven,
eager for men fated to die, shall speak much,
say to the eagle how he fared at the feasting,
when with the wolf he plundered the slain.'
Thus the man was the teller
of hateful tidings; he did not say much that was false
with respect to events and words. The troop all arose;
sorrowful they went under Earnanæs,
with welling tears, to gaze on the wonder.
Then, lifeless, on the sand, they found him
occupying his bed of rest, who, in former times,
gave them rings; then the hero's last day
had been reached, when the war-king,
the prince of the Weders, died a wondrous death.
First they saw there a remarkable creature,
the loathsome serpent, lying opposite
on the ground there, the fiery dragon,
terrible patterned horror, scorched with | live coals; [f.199v]
it was fifty feet in length
in the place of lying; it had joy of the sky
sometimes at night, then came back down
to visit its lair; now was it held fast in death,

hæfde eorðscrafa   ende genyttod.
Him big stodan   bunan ond orcas,
discas lagon   ond dryre swyrd,
omige þurhetone,   swa hie wið eorðan fæðm
þusend wintra   þær eardodon.
Þonne wæs þæt yrfe   eacencræftig,
iumonna gold   galdre bewunden,
þæt ðam hringsele   hrinan ne moste
gumena ænig   nefne God sylfa,
sigora Soðcyning   sealde þam ðe he wolde
—he is manna gehyld—   hord openian,
efne swa hwylcum manna   swa him gemet ðuhte.

XLII Þa wæs gesyne,   þæt se sið ne ðah
þam ðe unrihte   inne gehydde
wræ[t]e under wealle.   Weard ær onsloh
feara sumne;   þa sio fæhð geweard
gewrecen wraðlice.   Wundur hwar þonne
eorl ellenrof   ende gefere
lifgesceafta,   þonne leng ne mæg
mon mid his [ma]gum   meduseld buan.
Swa wæs Biowulfe, | þa he biorges weard   [f.200r]
sohte, searoniðas: seolfa ne cuðe
þurh hwæt his worulde gedal   weorðan sceolde.
Swa hit oð domes dæg   diope benemdon
þeodnas mære   þa ðæt þær dydon,
þæt se secg wære   synnum scildig,
hergum geheaðerod,   hellbendum fæst,
wommum gewitnad,   se ðone wong str[u]de;
næs he goldhwæte   gearwor hæfde
Agendes est   ær gesceawod.
   Wiglaf maðelode,   Wihstanes sunu:
'Oft sceall eorl monig   anes willan
wræc adreog[an],   swa us geworden is.
Ne meahton we gelæran   leofne þeoden,
rices hyrde   ræd ænigne,
þæt he ne grette   goldweard þone,
lete hyne licgean   þær he longe wæs,
wicum wunian   oð woruldende;
heold on heahgesceap.   Hord ys gesceawod,
grimme gegongen;   wæs þæt gifeðe to swið
þe ðone [þeodcyning]   þyder ontyhte.
Ic wæs þær inne   ond þæt eall geondseh,
recedes geatwa   þa me gerymed wæs,
nealles swæslice   sið alyfed
inn under eorðweall.   Ic on ofoste gefeng
micle mid mundum   mægenbyrðenne

had used its last earth-cavern.
Beside it stood drinking-vessels and cups,
dishes and precious swords lay
rusty, eaten through, just as they had remained there
in the bosom of the earth for a thousand years.
Then was that mighty heritage,
gold of men of a former age, encircled with a spell,
so that no man would be permitted to reach
that ring-hall, unless God himself,
the true king of victories —he is the protection of men—
had granted to whom he wished, to whatever man
might seem fitting to him, to open the hoard.
XLII Then was it manifest that the venture profited not
him who had wrongfully concealed the ornate object
under the earth-wall. The guardian had first slain
one of a few; then was the feud
grievously avenged. It is a mystery where
a brave eorl may reach the end
of his destined life, when he can no longer
dwell in the mead-hall with his kinsmen.
So was it for Beowulf, | when he sought out the guardian [f.200r]
of the barrow and his cunning enmity: he himself knew not
by what means his parting from the world was to come about.
In such a way famous princes who placed the treasure there
had solemnly declared that until doomsday,
the man who should plunder that place would be
guilty of sins, kept captive in the temples of idols,
held fast in hell's bonds, grievously tormented;
by no means had he previously perceived more fully
the gold-bestowing favour of the Lord.
Wiglaf spoke, son of Weohstan:
'Often must many an eorl endure misery
through the desire of one man, as has happened to us.
We could not persuade our beloved prince,
the guardian of the kingdom, by any counsel,
that he should not attack the guardian of gold,
but allow it to lie where it had long been,
to live in its dwelling-place until the world's end;
he kept his great destiny. The hoard has been examined,
grimly won; too strong was that fate
that impelled to that place [the people's king].
I was in there, and surveyed all that,
the precious trappings of the building, once the way was open to me;
not by any means in friendly fashion was passage granted me
beneath the mound. In haste I grasped
with my hands a huge load

hordgestreona, hider | ut ætbær [f.200v]
cyninge minum. Cwico wæs þa gena,
wis ond gewittig; worn eall gespræc
gomol on gehðo, ond eowic gretan het,
bæd þæt ge geworhton æfter wines dædum
in bælstede beorh þone hean,
micelne ond mærne, swa he manna wæs
wigend weorðfullost wide geond eorðan
þenden he burhwelan brucan moste.
Uton nu efstan oðre [siðe],
seon ond secean searo[gimma] geþræc,
wundur under wealle, ic eow wisige,
þæt ge genoge neon sceawiað
beagas ond brad gold. Sie sio bær gearo,
ædre geæfned þonne we ut cymen,
ond þonne geferian frean userne,
leofne mannan þær he longe sceal
on ðæs Waldendes wære geþolian.'
   Het ða gebeodan byre Wihstanes,
hæle hildedior, hæleða monegum,
boldagendra, þæt hie bælwudu
feorran feredon, folcagende,
godum togenes: 'Nu sceal gled fretan
—weaxan wonna leg— wigena strengel,
þone ðe oft gebad isernscure,
þonne stræla storm strengum gebæded
scoc ofer scildweall, sceft nytte heold,
fæ[ð]ergearwum fus flane fulleode.'
   Huru se snotra sunu Wihstanes
acigde of corðre | cyni[n]ges þegnas [f.201r]
syfone [æt]s*om*me, þa selestan,
eode eahta sum under inwithrof
hilderinc[a]; sum on handa bær
æledleoman, se ðe on orde geong.
Næs ða on hlytme, hwa þæt hord strude,
syððan orwearde ænigne dæl
secgas gesegon on sele wunian,
læne licgan; lyt ænig mearn
þæt hi ofostlic[e] ut geferedon
dyre maðmas; dracan ec scufun,
wyrm ofer weallclif, leton weg niman,
flod fæðmian frætwa hyrde.
Þ[a] wæs wunden gold on wæn hladen,
æghwæs unrim, æþelin[g] boren,
har hilde[rinc] to Hronesnæsse.
XLIII Him ða gegiredan Geata leode

of hoarded treasure, carried it away | out hither [f.200v]
to my king. He was then still alive,
alert and conscious; a great many things spoke
the old man in sorrow, and bade me greet you,
asked that ye should build, in remembrance of your friend's deeds,
at the site of the pyre, a high barrow,
huge and famous, just as of men he was
the most worthy warrior throughout the wide earth
while he was able to enjoy the wealth of a stronghold.
Let us now hasten to seek out and see
for a second time the pile of precious jewels,
the wonder beneath the walls; I shall guide you,
that ye from near at hand may look at sufficient
rings and broad gold. Let the bier be ready,
swiftly prepared, when we come out,
and then let us carry our lord,
the beloved man, to where he must long
abide in the keeping of the Ruler.'
   Then the son of Weohstan, the warrior bold in battle,
bade orders be given to many warriors, leaders of people,
men who owned halls, that from far off
they should bring wood for the pyre
of the valiant man: 'Now must live coals consume
—the fire grow dark— the ruler of warriors,
who oft endured the iron shower,
when driven from strings, the storm of arrows
passed over the shield-wall, the shaft did its duty,
hastening with feather flights, urged on the barb.'
   Well, the wise son of Weohstan
summoned, from the band of king's thanes, [f.201r]
the best seven together;
one of eight warriors, he went
beneath the evil roof; he who went in front
bore in his hand a torch.
There was no drawing of lots as to who would plunder the hoard,
once the men saw that any part
of it remained unguarded in the hall,
lay wasting away; little did anyone grieve
that they should hastily carry the precious treasures
outside; also they pushed the dragon,
the serpent, over the cliff, let the wave take it,
the flood enfold the keeper of ornaments.
Then was a countless number of everything
of twisted gold loaded on a wagon and the ætheling,
the grey-haired warrior, borne to Hronesness.

XLIII The people of the Geats made ready for him

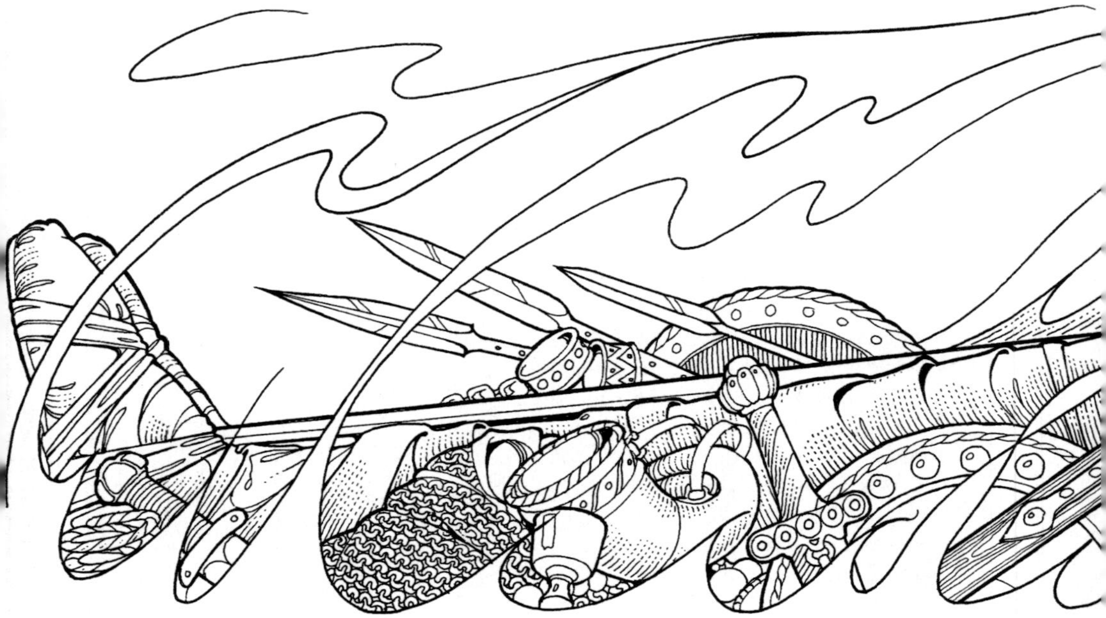

ad on eorðan unwaclicne,
helm[um] behongen, hildebordum,
beorhtum byrnum, swa he bena wæs;
alegdon ða tomiddes mærne þeoden
hæleð hiofende, hlaford leofne.
Ongunnon þa on beorge bælfyra mæst
wigend weccan; wud[u]rec astah
sweart ofer swi[o]ðole, swogende le[g]
wope bewunden —windblond gelæg—
oðþæt he ða banhus gebrocen hæfde,
hat on hreðre. Higum unrote
modceare mændon, mondryhtnes cw[e]alm.
Swylce giomorgyd | [G]*e*at[isc] meowle [f.201v]
[. . . . .] *b*undenhe*o*rde
[so]*ng* sorgcearig; sæ[d]e geneahhe
þæt hio hyre [here]g[a]*n*gas hearde *ond*[r]*e*de,
wælfylla wo*rn*, *weru*des egesan,
hy[n]ðo ond h*æf*[t]*nyd*. Heofon rece swealg.
Geworhton ða Wedra leode
hl*æw* on *ho*e, se [w]æs heah ond brad,
[wæ]gliðendum wide g[e]syne,
ond beti[m]bredon on tyn dagum
beadurofes becn, bronda l*afe*
wealle beworhton, swa hyt weorðlicost
foresnotre men findan mihton.
Hi on beorg dydon beg ond siglu,
eall swylce hyrsta swylce on horde ær
niðhedige men genumen hæfdon;

a splendid funeral pyre on the ground,
hung round with helmets, battle-shields,
bright byrnies, as he had requested;
then, lamenting, the warriors laid in its midst
the famous prince, their beloved lord.
The warriors began to kindle on the cliff
the greatest of funeral fires; the wood-reek rose up,
black above the fire; the roaring flame
mingled with weeping —the swirling wind subsided—
until it had broken the bone-house,
hot at its heart. Sad in spirit,
they lamented their grief, the slaying of their liege lord.
Likewise the Geatish woman, [f.201v]
[..................] with hair bound up,
sang a sorrowful song; said repeatedly
that she herself sorely dreaded army invasions,
a multitude of slaughters, the terror of troops,
humiliation and captivity. Heaven swallowed up the smoke.
Then the people of the Geats built
a burial-mound on the headland, high and broad,
widely visible by seafarers,
and in ten days they built the monument
for the brave in battle, the remnants from the flames
they built round with a wall, as most worthily
very wise men could devise.
In the barrow they placed rings and jewels,
all such adornments as hostile-minded men
had earlier taken from the hoard;

forleton eorla gestreon   eorðan healdan,
gold on greote,   þær hit nu gen lifað
eldum swa unnyt   swa h*i*[t ær]*or* wæs.
Þa ymbe hlæw riodan   hilded*i*ore,
æþelinga bearn,   ealra twelf[e],
woldon [ceare] cwiðan   [ond] kyning mænan,
wordgyd wrecan   ond ymb w[er] sprecan;
eahtodan eorlscipe   ond his ellenweorc
duguðum demdon,   swa hit ged[efe] bið
þæt mon his winedryhten   wordum herge,
ferhðum freog[e],   þonne he forð scile
of lichaman   [læded] weorðan.
Swa begnornodon   Geata leode
hlafordes [hr]*y*re,   heorðgeneatas;
cwædon þæt he wære   wyruldcyning[a]
mann*um* mildust   ond mon[ðw]ærust,
leodum liðost   ond lofgeornost.

they let the earth keep the wealth of eorls,
gold in the earth, where now it still exists,
as useless to men as it was previously.
Then men brave in battle, sons of æthelings,
rode round the barrow; twelve in all,
they would lament their loss, mourn their king,
utter a dirge, and speak about the man;
they praised his heroism and judged highly
his courageous deed; so it is fitting
that one praise his friend and lord with words,
heartily love him, when he must be led forth
from his body and pass away.
Thus did the people of the Geats,
his hearth-companions, lament the fall of their lord;
said that of earthly kings he had been
the gentlest and most gracious of men,
kindest to his people, and most eager for fame.

BOB FARLEY

THE FIGHT AT FINNSBURH

THE FIGHT AT FINNSBURH

'. . . . . [hor]nas byrnað?'
[H]næ[f] hleoþrode ða, hea[þ]ogeong cyning:
'Ne ðis ne dagað east[a]n, ne her draca ne fleogeð,
ne her ðisse healle, hornas ne byrnað;
ac her forþ berað, fugelas singað,
gylleð græghama, guðwudu hlynneð,
scyld scefte oncwyð. Nu scyneð þes mona
waðol under wolcnum; nu arisað weadæda,
ðe ðisne folces nið fremman willað.
Ac onwacnigeað nu, wigend mine,
habbað eowre l[i]nda, hi[c]geaþ on ellen,
win[n]að on orde, wesað on mode!'
Ða aras mænig goldhladen ðegn, gyrde hine his swurde;
ða to dura eodon drihtlice cempan,
Sigeferð and Eaha, hyra sword getugon,
and æt oþrum durum Ordlaf and Guþlaf,
and Hengest sylf hwearf him on laste.
Ða gyt Garulf Guðere sty[r]de,
ðæt he swa freolic feorh forman siþe
to ðære healle durum hyrsta ne bær[e],
nu hyt niþa heard anyman wolde;
ac he frægn ofer eal undearninga,
deormod hæleþ, hwa ða duru heolde.
'Sigeferþ is min nama,' cweþ he, 'ic eom Secgena leod,
wrec[c]e[a] wide cuð; fæla ic we[a]na gebad,
he[a]rdra hilda; ðe is gyt her witod,
swæþer ðu sylf to me secean wylle.'
Ða wæs on healle wælslihta gehlyn:
sceolde cel[lod] bor[d] [c]enum on handa
banhelm berstan; buruhðelu dynede,
oð æt ðære guðe Garulf gecrang
ealra ærest eorðbuendra,
Guðlafes sunu, ymbe hyne godra fæla,
hwearfl[i]cra hræ[w]. Hræfn wandrode
sweart and sealobrun. Swurdleoma stod,
swylce eal Finnsburuh fyrenu wære,
ne gefrægn ic næfre wurþlicor æt wera hilde
sixtig sigebeorna sel gebæra[n],
ne nefre swan[as] hwitne medo sel forgyldan,

THE FIGHT AT FINNSBURH

.... gables burn?'
   Then spoke Hnæf, the king young in war:
'This is no dawning from the east, nor here does dragon fly,
nor here do this hall's gables burn;
but hither they bear forth [weapons], birds are calling out,
the grey-coated [one] is baying; spear resounds,
shield answers shaft. Now shines this moon,
wandering beneath clouds; now begin deeds of woe
that will bring about this enmity of the people.
But, awaken now, my warriors,
hold fast your shields, think of valour,
fight in the front, be of courage!'
   Then arose many a gold-adorned thane, girded on his sword;
and to the door the noble warriors went,
Sigeferth and Eaha, and drew their swords,
and at the other door(s) Ordlaf and Guthlaf,
and Hengest himself followed in their track.
Garulf still restrained Guthhere,
that he, so noble a life, at the first onset [of the attack],
should not bear his armour to the door of the hall,
now that a warrior fierce in battle wished to deprive him of it;
but the bold-spirited warrior, over it all,
asked openly who guarded the door.
'Sigeferth is my name,' said he, 'I am a man of the Secgas,
a widely-known exile; many woes have I experienced,
fierce battles; yet here is already decreed for thee
whichever outcome thou thyself may wish to seek from me.'
   Then was there din of slaughter in hall;
brave hands grasped hollow shields,
bone-protectors shattered, hall-floor resounded
until Garulf fell in that fight,
first of all dwellers on earth,
Guthlaf's son, around him many heroes,
active bodies. The raven circled round,
black and dusky brown. The sword-light gleamed,
as if all Finnsburh were on fire.
Never have I heard tell of sixty victorious warriors
behaving more honourably in battle,
nor ever young men repaying better the bright mead

ðonne Hnæfe guldan his hægstealdas.
Hig fuhton fif dagas, swa hyra nan ne feol,
drihtgesiða, ac hig ða duru heoldon.
Ða gewat him wund hæleð on wæg gangan,
sæde þæt his byrne abrocen wære,
heresceorp u[n]hror, and eac wæs his helm ðyr[e]l.
Ða hine sona frægn folces hyrde
hu ða wigend hyra wunda genæson,
oððe hwæþer ðæra hyssa . . . .

than his young men had repaid Hnæf.
Five days they fought, so that none fell
of the companions, but they held the doors.
  Then a wounded warrior went away,
said his corselet was broken into pieces,
his armour weak, and his helmet pierced through.
Then at once the people's guardian asked him
how the warriors survived their wounds,
or whether [any] of the youths . . . .

NOTES AND COMMENTARY

Beowulf [Selected passages]

Of Scyld [1–52]

The poem begins with a reference to the glory and prowess of the Danish chiefs in ancient tradition.

Of these chiefs, Scyld, who came to the Danes as a helpless foundling, is especially mentioned as a successful conqueror, since he had subjugated all the neighbouring princes, including those across the sea. Scyld has a son, Beowulf, who succeeds him in his declining years, when his strength is beginning to fail. The poet moralizes.

Then, after a long reign and about to die, Scyld, at his own request, was taken to the sea-shore by his retainers and despatched to sea in a ship filled with costly armour and other treasures, to do him honour, as befitted a true sea-king and one who, as a child, had been sent forth to sea alone in like manner.

4 Scyld (also 19, 26), mythical Danish king Scefing, Scyld's epithet, meaning 'with a sheaf', came to be regarded by folk-etymology as 'Son of Scef' or 'Sceaf' owing to confusion with the patronymic *-ing* at a time when the original had been forgotten. Hence the Sceaf of the genealogies.

18 Beowulf, Danish king, son of Scyld, is apparently the Beow or Beowa of the West Saxon and other genealogies and may have been miswritten by a scribe confusing him with Beowulf the Geat, the hero of the poem. This Beowulf is the father of Healfdene, and grandfather of Hrothgar, whose hall the Geat hero is to free from Grendel's attacks and is never mentioned again after the Scyld episode.

30 Scyldings (*passim*), descendants of Scyld, the Danish royal family.

Beowulf's Swimming Match with Breca [499–606]

After an exchange of courtesies between Beowulf and Hrothgar and the latter's acceptance of the hero's offer to rid Heorot of the monster Grendel, the benches are cleared, ale is drunk freely, and a scop sings clear-voiced to the assembled company, for an end to the depredations of their envious foe seems almost inevitable. Now comes a jarring note. Unferth, a Danish courtier, overcome by jealousy, taunts Beowulf.

'Art thou that Beowulf,' he says, 'who strove with Breca in swimming in the open sea in winter, for seven days, and got beaten? A worse fate lies in store for thee when thou meetest Grendel!'

Beowulf replies with much warmth, giving his own version of the story about Breca. When they were young men, he and Breca had dared each other to a swimming-match on the sea, each taking a naked sword as a protection against whales. They kept together for five days, until cold and darkness and the high wind separated them. Then a sea-monster attacked Beowulf and dragged him down. But, he was protected by his armour and despatched the beast.

More of the sea-beasts came on. Beowulf laid about him with his sword and slew nine of them. Their mutilated corpses strewed the shore. Then the sun rose and Beowulf could see the land. Never had there been a tougher struggle; but fortune often favours the undoomed brave; and Beowulf lived through it. He was landed at last by the current on the shore of the country of the Lapps, exhausted, but safe.

'I have never,' adds Beowulf, 'heard any such exploits told about thee, Unferth! Neither thou nor Breca are equal to it. It is true thou didst kill thy own brothers; but thou wilt have to suffer for that in hell, clever as thou art. The fact is, Grendel would never have wrought such mischief if thou and thy Danish comrades had not been such cowards. As it is, he does as he pleases, and cares not a straw for your warlike Danes.'

499 Unferth (also 530), a Dane; a literary creation ('Unpeace') as the name suggests, rather than a historical person; spokesman and trusted adviser to Hrothgar; said to have slain his brother; lends Beowulf his sword *Hrunting* for the fight against Grendel's mother; serves the poet not only as a foil to Beowulf but also to bring out certain points in the hero's character. Ecglaf (also 590), father of Unferth.

501 Beowulf (*passim*), the hero, son of Ecgtheow the Wægmunding; a Geat, sister's son to the historical king Hygelac of Geatland; later himself King of the Geats.

506 Breca (also 531, 583), son of Beanstan and chief of the Brondings (see *Widsith* 25).

519 Heathoremes, tribe of Norway.

521 Brondings, unidentified tribal name.

524 Beanstan, father of Breca.

527 Grendel (*passim*), a monster of the marshes.

529 Ecgtheow (also 1651, 2587), father of Beowulf; a Wægmunding; marries the only daughter of Hrethel, King of the Geats; slays the Wylfing, Heatholaf; escapes to Denmark, where Hrothgar pays his *wergild*.

The Tale of Sigemund [874b–97]

Grendel's arm is wrenched off by Beowulf during their fight in Heorot and the monster leaves a trail of blood on his way back to his underwater lair. The mere, on receiving him into its clasp, boils with blood –the frightful surge of the waves welling up. Those of Hrothgar's warriors who had gone to see the strange sight, ride back boldly, praising Beowulf's great feat. On the way, the scop improvises a lay in honour of Beowulf and compares him to Sigemund and Heremod. He mentions Sigemund's fight against the giants (undertaken together with his nephew Fitela) and his successful dragon fight. Indeed, Sigemund was the most famous warrior since Heremod's death. The latter, though he had raised great expectations, became cruel and tyrannous and was hated by his people, whereas everyone loves Beowulf.

In its cursory, epitomizing form, this 'Tale' embodies two separate stories going back, possibly, to two originally distinct lays: (i) Sigemund's *wide siðas* of fierce fighting, especially those undertaken in company with Fitela, and (ii) his dragon fight.

According to the *Volsungasaga* (chapters 3–8), Sigmundr is the eldest son of King Volsungr, a descendant of Oþinn. Sigmundr's twin sister, Signý, is married against her will to Siggeirr, King of Gautland. While on a visit at Siggeirr's court, Volsungr and his men are treacherously slain; his sons are captured and killed one after another except Sigmundr, who escapes into the forest. Sigmundr and Signý brood revenge. Seeing that her sons by Siggeirr are lacking in valour and that only a true Volsung son will be able to help in the work of revenge, Signý, impelled by a desperate resolve, disguises herself as a witch and visits her brother in the forest. When her time comes, she gives birth to a son, who is named Sinfjotli. At his mother's bidding, when he is ten years old, the boy joins Sigmundr (who does not know until the final catastrophe that Sinfjotli is his son) and is trained by him in deeds of strength and endurance. Finally Sigmundr and Sinfjotli together accomplish the revenge by setting fire to Siggeirr's hall. How far the version known to the author of *Beowulf* agreed with this part of the *Volsungasaga*, it is impossible to determine. The fact that Fitela is referred to as Sigemund's *nefa* only (881), might perhaps be held to indicate Sigemund's ignorance of their true relationship, or it may be attributed to the Christian author's desire to suppress what was considered a morally revolting motive. But we do not know, indeed, whether the Anglo-Saxons of that time were at all acquainted with the story answering to the Sigmundr-Signý motif. The form *Fitela* differs from the established Norse compound name *Sinfjotli* and from the High German *Sintarfizzilo*. Also, the designation of Sigemund's father as *Wæls* (897) differs from his Norse name *Volsungr*, which latter is presumably the result of confusion, the patronymic form being taken for a proper name.

Sigemund's dragon fight is peculiar to *Beowulf*. It naturally suggests the famous dragon fight of his still greater son (Old Norse *Sigurðr*, Middle High German *Sigfrit*) which roused the imagination of the Scandinavians and was not forgotten by the Germans, and which in fact –especially as part of the great *Nibelungen* cycle– has been celebrated in modern Germanic epic, drama, and music. But there are differences between the two stories, quite apart from the greater fullness of detail found in the narrative of Sigurðr's exploit. The manner of the fight itself is not the same, Sigemund's deed appearing the more genuinely heroic one. Noteworthy incidents of the *Beowulf* version are the dissolving of the dragon in its own heat (897) and the carrying away of the hoard in a boat (895). It is widely held that the dragon fight belongs properly to Sigfrit and not to Sigemund, his father, yet there is no positive evidence to prove that the Anglo-Saxon poet was wrong when he attributed that exploit to the latter. Sigurðr-Sigfrit may, in fact, have been unknown to him. It is, on the whole, probable that in his allusions to Sigemund, as well as to Heremod, he followed Danish tradition, and that no connexion had yet been established between the Sigemund (*Wælsing*) legends and those of Sigfrit and of the Burgundians.

875 Sigemund (also 884), son of Wæls and (at least in Norse tradition) father and uncle of Fitela.
877 Wælsing, son of Wæls, that is, Sigemund.
879 Fitela (also 889), son and nephew of Sigemund, the dragon-slayer.
897 Wæls, father of Sigemund

The Tale of Finn [1063–1159a]

In the course of a brilliant ceremony at Heorot in honour of Beowulf's victory, the hero is offered rich presents by the king in addition to gold for the loss of the man whom Grendel devoured. There is singing and music and as part of the entertainment Hrothgar's scop recites the 'Tale of Finn' which is about a band of sixty Danes under their chief Hnæf who find themselves attacked before daybreak in the hall of the Frisian king Finn, whom they have come to visit ... Five days they fight without loss against the Frisians, but at the end Hnæf and many of his men, as well as of the Frisians, are slain. Finn is forced to conclude a treaty with Hengest, who has now assumed command over the Danes. The fallen warriors of both tribes are burned together amid appropriate ceremonies and Hengest and his men remain in Friesland during the winter. Deep in his heart, however, Hengest yearns for revenge. The day of reckoning comes when the Danes Guthlaf and Oslaf, unable any longer to keep the silence imposed upon them by the terms of the treaty, openly rebuke their old foes. Finn is attacked and slain, and his queen, Hildeburh, together with the royal treasure of the Frisians, is carried back to the land of the Danes.

This 'Tale' is twice alluded to in *Beowulf* (in some detail, 1069 ff., and only briefly, 1151 ff.). For a resolution of some of the obscurities of the Finn Legend we must turn, however, to the *Finnsburh Fragment* [see L J Rodrigues, *Three Anglo-Saxon Battle Poems*, Llanerch, 1996], as it is obvious that the latter poem not only describes the events connected with the 'Tale' but also precedes it. The antecedents to the conflict are lost to us. But evidently Hildeburh is in some way connected with the hostility between her brother and her husband. There may have existed an old feud between the two tribes, and the Danish princess had been given in marriage to the Frisian king in the hope of securing permanent peace, but with the same grievous result as in the case of Freawaru. Or the ill feeling may have dated from the wedding feast (as in the *Volsungasaga*, chapter 3). It is possible also –though far from probable– that Hildeburh had been abducted like Hildr, Hogni's daughter, in Snorri's *Edda* and Hilde, Hagene's daughter in the Middle High German epic of *Kudrun*. At any rate, at least fifteen or twenty years must have elapsed after the marriage, since Hildeburh's son falls in the battle (1074, 1115).

1064 Healfdene (also 1652, 1866), King of the Danes, succeeding his father Beowulf, son of Scyld; reigned very happily, and had four children: Heorogar, Hrothgar, and Halga, and a daughter whose name has been lost.
1066 Hrothgar, son of Healfdene, builder of Heorot.
1068 Finn (also 1081, 1096, 1128, 1146, 1152, 1156), King of the East Frisians and also the Jutes; son of Folcwalda; married to Hildeburh, a Half-Dane.

1069 Hnæf (also 1114), leader of the Half-Danes, killed at Finnsburh by the Frisians. Half-Danes, a Danish tribe to which Hoc, Hnæf and Hildeburh belonged.

1070 Fri(e)sians (also 1093, 1104), a Germanic tribe whose language is closer to English than other Low German dialects.

1071 Hildeburh (also 1114), Finn's Queen of Friesland, daughter of Hoc the Half-Dane, sister of Hnæf.

1072 Jutes (also 1088, 1141, 1145), followers of Finn and the Frisians.

1076 Hoc, King of the Half-Danes, father of Hnæf and Hildeburh.

1083 Hengest (also 1091, 1096, 1127), a Half-Dane who succeeded Hnæf to the leadership after the Frisian attack on the hall at Finnsburh.

1089 Folcwalda, father of Finn, the Frisian.

1126 Friesland, land of the Fri(e)sians. In the East, Finn's kingdom; in the West, allied with the Franks against Hygelac.

1143 Hunlaf, probably the father of Guthlaf and Oslaf. The weapon, according to the Anglo-Saxon poet, is a famous sword, 'best of battle-blades', which, like *Hrunting* and *Nægling* (*Beowulf* 1490 and 2680), or *Mimming* (*Waldere*, I, 3) belongs to Germanic story.

1148 It is not clear from the story whether Guthlaf and Oslaf were the sons of Hunlaf or merely followers of Hnæf.

The Vengeance of Grendel's Mother [1251–1309]

After the banquet is over, Hrothgar retires to his chamber, and the hall is cleared for sleeping. At each man's head is laid his armour, as is the custom, so that they might be ready for night-attacks or surprises. Thus they go to sleep –a sleep which costs one of them his life! Rumour is rife that another monster still lives, of whom Grendel is the offspring. This creature broods over the loss of Grendel, whose origin is again referred to, as is his defeat by Beowulf.

Grendel's mother resolves to go to Heorot and avenge his death. Terror again seizes the hall-dwellers, though less than in Grendel's case, as might well have been expected when a woman is in question. The warriors hurriedly seize their swords; there is no time to put on armour. The monster snatches up one of the men (Æschere, a high favourite of Hrothgar) and makes off with him to the fens. Beowulf is not there; another sleeping-place had been assigned to him. A wail of anguish goes up from Heorot, and Hrothgar is again overwhelmed with grief.

1261 Cain, brother of Abel, Genesis iv (see 111).

1267 Heorot (*passim*), Hrothgar's magnificent hall, built after he becomes King of Denmark, scene of Beowulf's fight with Grendel; situated probably near the ancient Hleiðr, modern Lejre, on the north coast of Zealand and a little to the south-east of Roskilde.

Hrothgar's Description of the Monsters and their Lair [1345–76b]

Beowulf is hastily summoned into Hrothgar's presence and told what has happened to Æschere. Hrothgar, lamenting the loss of his trusted retainer and a resumption of the conflict against evil in the person of Grendel's mother, tells Beowulf that he, too, had heard that there were two monsters –one a female– who stalked the moors. In a graphic passage he goes on to describe their haunt, a gloomy mere not far distant, over which a sort of will-o'-the-wisp hovers at night. Rather than plunge into it, the hart chased by hounds will die on the bank.

Beowulf's Fight with Grendel's Mother [1495b–1549]

Beowulf accedes to Hrothgar's appeal for help and an expedition to the mere is undertaken immediately. The trail of blood left by the monster is followed down to the mere where they behold Æschere's head lying on a cliff beside the blood-stained waters. Beowulf is determined to fight the hag and goes down into the mere armed with *Hrunting*, the sword lent him by Unferth. But it is a good part of the day before he reaches the bottom. Grendel's mother becomes aware that her retreat is being invaded. She clutches at him, but his trusty harness protects him, and he comes to no harm. However, she drags him downwards to her lair. He is greatly hindered in using his weapons, and in swimming, by the clasp of his adversary and the attacks of other water-creatures.

At last he comes to a cavern to which the water has no access, and by the lurid flame within he sees the mere-wife and deals her a desperate blow with his sword. But for the first time the weapon fails –it glances back from the monster's head.

Undaunted, Beowulf flings aside the sword and trusts to his mighty hand-grip. Seizing the monster by the shoulder, he flings her to the ground but stumbles in doing so and she quickly pins him down. She draws her dagger but cannot pierce his armour –God and his war-corselet protect him, and he stands upright once more.

Beowulf brings back Grendel's Head [1572b–1676]

Then, sword in hand, Beowulf examines the vault and comes across the carcass of Grendel, whose head he cuts off.

The onlookers on the bank of the mere now observe that its waters are troubled and stained with blood. They give way to gloomy forebodings, and at three o'clock in the afternoon Hrothgar and his Danes return home, leaving Beowulf's little band of followers still faithfully waiting for their lord, but almost in despair.

Beowulf takes nothing from the cave except Grendel's head and the hilt of the sword –for the blade had been dissolved by the monster's poisonous blood.

Soon he is swimming upwards again through the now purified waters, and lands amid the rejoicings of his company. He is relieved of his armour by the side of the now calm lake, and his followers return with him to Hrothgar's hall, radiant with victory. Four of them have hard work to carry the monster's head on a pole.

Beowulf enters the hall in triumph to greet Hrothgar. Grendel's head is also brought into the hall –a thing of horror to the queen and the assembled nobles.

Beowulf lays before the king his trophies –the monster's head and the sword-hilt– and relates how narrowly he escaped defeat and death, how *Hrunting* failed him in his hour of need, and how he was guided by the good providence of God to see another sword hanging on the wall of the chamber, with which he slew Grendel's mother and cut off the head of the dead Grendel as well. As the sword-blade was completely eaten away by the blood of the two water-creatures,

Beowulf could only bring away the hilt as a trophy. Now is the slaughter of the Danes avenged; now may Hrothgar sleep fearlessly in Heorot, quiet and secure as at the beginning.

1659 *Hrunting*, Unferth's famous sword, loaned to Beowulf.

Hrothgar's Homiletic Oration [1700–84]

The golden hilt is handed to and examined by Hrothgar; it has graven upon it the destruction of the race of giants by the flood, and an inscription in runic letters showing for whom it had been made.

Hrothgar affirms the pre-eminence of Beowulf, admires his bearing, and confirms his promises towards him. He refers to the behaviour of the Danish king Heremod, a cruel and ungenerous tyrant, and a contrast to that of Beowulf.

Heremod's history points a moral. God sometimes gives a man great prosperity –everything seems in his favour until a time comes when his sense of what is due to others becomes torpid, to his great peril, and arrogance takes a hold of him, He cannot resist the promptings of the devil. All he has seems too little. He covets, and neglects the great duty of giving, forgetful of God's bounty to him and of his future state. One day he drops out of his place, and is succeeded by another who wins a well-earned security by lavish gifts.

So Hrothgar exhorts Beowulf not to be arrogant or unmindful (like Heremod) of the future. His time of glory will last for a while, and then death will come. He himself had been king for fifty years, prosperous and happy; and then Grendel suddenly appeared –a constant trouble. But now, thank God, he is permitted to look upon the monster's head.

He bids Beowulf take part in the banqueting and promises him much treasure on the morrow.

1709 Heremod, Danish king, after whose death in exile, it would seem, Scyld Scefing was mysteriously sent to build up the Danish state; hence he occurs just above Scyld in the Anglo-Saxon genealogies; serves the poet as a foil to both Hrothgar and Beowulf in two moralizing passages in the poem (here, and at 901 ff.).

1710 Ecgwela, an unknown Danish king.

Beowulf Returns Home [1866–1919]

The aged king gives Beowulf twelve costly gifts and weeps at his leave-taking, overcome with emotion at the thought that he may never see him again. So Beowulf, rejoicing in the rich bounty of the king, sets off, accompanied by his men. All praise Hrothgar's generosity.

At the water's edge, they encounter the coastguard, whose courteous behaviour is rewarded by a sword from Beowulf. They load the ship with their armour and presents and depart, and after a prosperous voyage arrive at the land of the Geats.

The harbour-guard hurries to the beach, from which he had so often gazed seawards in the hope of sighting Beowulf's ship, and makes fast the craft to the shore.

The Tale of (Mod)thryth [1931b–62]

Beowulf returns to Geatland with his comrades. They have landed safely and are on their way to the royal hall where Hygelac resides with his young wife Hygd. Though she has not reigned long, she has proved a generous queen. (Mod)thryth –and here the digression abruptly begins– perpetrated terrible deeds. No man dared look at her for fear of being put to death immediately. 'Ne bið swylc cwenlic þeaw idese to efnanne,' the poet says. On her father's bidding, she had sailed to the court of Offa and no sooner had she married him than she gave up her violent ways, and became a generous queen at the side of Offa, who was himself a brave and excellent ruler. They had a son called Eomer.

Despite her youth, Hygd, Hrothgar's wife, shows the virtues of a discreet woman and a gracious, generous queen, differing thus from (Mod)thryth in her early pre-marital stage; and, in his 'Tale of (Mod)thryth', the scop probably intends this remarkable woman to represent a haughty, violent maiden, who cruelly has any man put to death who is bold enough merely to look at her fair face (1941), but who, after being wedded to the right husband, becomes an admirable, womanly wife (and kind, generous [1952] queen).

Offa, who while still young (1948) married the noble (1949), impetuous maiden, is extolled (1955 ff.) as the most excellent hero, famed for his valour, wisdom, and liberality. He is the son of Garmund and the father of Eomer, and corresponds to the legendary, pre-historic Anglian king Offa I of the Mercian genealogies. Being removed twelve generations from the historical Offa II, the old Anglian Offa may be assigned to the latter half of the fourth century. His great exploit is the single combat by the river Eider alluded to in *Widsith* (35 ff.).

The stories concerning both Offa and (Mod)thryth undoubtedly arose in the ancient continental home of the Angles. The Offa tradition lived on for centuries among the Danes, and it appears in literary, nationalized form (Warmundus figuring as the king of Denmark) in the pages of Saxo Grammaticus and Sven Åageson. On the other hand, the Angles migrating to Britain carried the legends of Offa and his queen with them and in course of time localized them in their new home. Offa I became the *Vita* king of the West Angles (Mercians), the founder of the city of Warwick, and considerable confusion between the two Offas set in, leading to further variations.

1931 (Mod)thryth, wife of the Anglian king Offa.

1944 Hemming (also 1961), an Angle, kinsman of Offa and Eomer (or Eomær).

1949 Offa (also 1957), king of the Continental Angles.

1960 Eomer, Anglian prince, son of Offa, grandson of Garmund, and kinsman of Hemming.

1962 Garmund, father of the Anglian king Offa.

The Tale of Freawaru [2024b–69a]

In his report to Hygelac Beowulf describes his reception at Heorot and alludes to the king's daughter, Freawaru, who distributed the ale-cups to the *dugoðe*.

The young princess is betrothed to Frotha's son, Ingeld, in an effort to put an end to the interminable feud between Danes and Heathobards. Beowulf warns that such a settlement is bound to be transient; the followers of Freawaru will carry swords that once belonged to Heathobard warriors who had been killed in battle (by the Danes), and the Heathobards will resent it. Then, 'an aged spearsman, who eyes a ring-hilt, remembers it all, the spear-death of heroes' (2041–3). He incites a young comrade, whose father's sword is now borne by a Dane in the Heathobards' hall, to an act of revenge. Again and again he spurs him on with bitter words until the young man kills Freawaru's thane. Retaliation will follow on the part of the Danes and this will kindle Ingeld's *wælniðas* whereas his love for his wife will grow cold. So, Beowulf concludes, 'I hold hollow the Heathobards' lordly alliance with loyal Danes, a specious friendship' (2067–9).

Saxo's version of the Heathobard episode [*Gesta Danorum*, trans. O. Elton (London, 1894), bk.vi, 182 ff.] and the 'Tale of Freawaru' is as follows. Frotho, who succeeded to the Danish throne when he was in his twelfth year, overcame and subjected the Saxon kings Swerting and Hanef. He proved an excellent king, strong in war, generous, virtuous, and honourable. Meanwhile Swerting, anxious to throw off the Danish yoke, treacherously resolved to slay Frotho, who forestalled and slew him, but was slain by him simultaneously. Frotho was succeeded by his son Ingellus, whose soul was perverted from honour. Forsaking the examples of his forefathers, he indulged in wanton profligacy. He married the daughter of Swerting given him by her brothers, who desired to insure themselves against the Danish king's vengeance. When Starcatherus, the former guardian of Frotho's son, heard that Ingellus was perversely minded, and instead of punishing his father's murderers, bestowed kindness and friendship upon them, he was vexed with stinging wrath at the heinousness of the crime. He returned from his wanderings in foreign lands, where he had been fighting, and clad in mean attire, betook himself to the royal hall and awaited the king. In the evening, Ingellus took his meal with the sons of Swerting, and enjoyed a magnificent feast. The tables had been loaded with the profusest dishes. The stern guest soon recognized by the king, violently spurned the queen's efforts to please him, and when he saw that Frotho's slayers were in high favour with the king, he could not refrain from attacking Ingellus's character, but poured out the whole bitterness of his reproaches on his head, to which he added a song that so roused Ingellus by its earnest admonition that he leapt up, drew his sword, and straightway slew the sons of Swerting.

Compared with the version in *Beowulf*, Saxo's marks an advance in dramatic power in that the climax is brought about by a single act (not by exhortations made on several occasions, *mæla gehwylce* 2057), and that Ingellus himself carries out the vengeance, whereas in the Anglo-Saxon poem the slaying of one of the queen's retinue by an unnamed warrior provokes the catastrophe.

2025 Froda (or Frotho), king of Denmark, father of Ingeld, the husband of Freawaru.

2032 Heathobard (also 2037, 2067), a Germanic tribe whose king was Ingeld.

2052 Withergyld, a Heathobard warrior.

2064 Ingeld, son of Froda, king of the Heathobards, married Freawaru, Hrothgar's daughter.

The Lament of the Last Survivor [2247–66]
The man who first came upon the hoard was an outlaw who sought refuge in the cave. He is astonished at the wealth of treasure round him – the rich spoils of a past generation of warriors, placed there by the last survivor of a noble company, who laments his loneliness in a memorable elegy.

The Dragon [2270b–2344]
The hoard was unprotected when discovered by the dragon. Although of no particular good to him, the monster decides to mount guard over it. The outlaw steals a precious goblet and buys the favour of his lord with it. The hoard is ransacked. The dragon awakes, and becomes aware that an enemy has been in his cave, and despoiled him of treasure. He waits for the night in order to take vengeance, and then ravages the country with fire. The whole countryside is consumed by the fire from the dragon's mouth; even Beowulf's stronghold is attacked by the flames. He fears that he must have displeased almighty God, and is greatly dejected. He has a fireproof shield of iron made for himself, and disdaining the help of an army, determines to fight the dragon single-handed, no less daring in his old age than when he quelled Grendel and his monster mother.

A Father's Lament for his Son [2444–62a]
Seated upon a headland, full of gloomy forebodings, Beowulf makes a farewell speech to the twelve companions he has chosen to accompany him on this exploit. First he tells how in his early youth he was a favourite at King Hrethel's court; how Hæthcyn, one of the king's sons, accidentally slew Herebeald, his elder brother, whose death remained unavenged, since Hrethel was forbidden, by the code of kinship, to kill or exact vengeance from a kinsman; and then, in an elegaic passage, he portrays the piteous case of a father who loses his son by a violent death.

Beowulf and Wiglaf Slay the Dragon and Beowulf's Death [2510–2891]
Beowulf announces his intention of going forth at once to the fight. He will not disdain armour as he did when fighting Grendel, but will take a shield and corselet to protect himself against the fire-breathing dragon. He will conquer single-handed or die. His comrades are to keep watch on the barrow.

Beowulf advances to the cave and challenges the dragon. The latter comes forth, spewing flame. Beowulf draws his sword, and waits for the dragon's attack. As he comes forward, the king deals him a blow with his sword, though not such a mighty one as he wished. The reptile belches forth more flame, and still the sword fails its owner in his need.

He is seen to be in difficulty by his little company; but they retreat, panic-stricken, into a neighbouring wood. One of the company, Wiglaf, remembering the favours he had had from Beowulf, is struck with remorse, and prepares to join in the fray.

There follows the history of Wiglaf's sword. Weohstan, his father, had taken it from Onela's nephew Eanmund, whom he had slain and kept it until his son Wiglaf was grown to man's estate, when he handed it down to him. This is the first time

Wiglaf has fought by the side of Beowulf; his courage is good and his sword proves trusty.

Before he goes, he rebukes his comrades for their ingratitude and cowardice in the hour of need. For his part, he will share the fortunes of war with his lord. On joining Beowulf, he encourages him to do his best, and assures him of his help.

The dragon attacks Wiglaf, and Beowulf drives his sword *Nægling* into the monster's head; but it snaps, and the dragon gives him a deadly bite in the neck. The blood gushes out in torrents. Wiglaf wounds the dragon and the fire from him abates; the king revives for a short time and cuts the reptile asunder.

It becomes evident that Beowulf's wound is mortal. Wiglaf bathes it, and undoes his armour. Then Beowulf, feeling that death is near, grieves that he has no son to whom he may leave his armour. He comforts himself with the thought of his upright life, and asks Wiglaf to bring the treasure out of the cave, that he may have the last joy of gazing upon it.

Wiglaf enters the vault and sees the treasure, rusted and dull, but of great value. The cavern is lit up by a wondrous gleaming banner, which Wiglaf carries off, together with a load of goblets and dishes. He hastens back to Beowulf, fearing that he may not find him alive. Beowulf is, indeed, at the last gasp: but, after being refreshed with water, is able to make a dying speech.

Beowulf thanks God that he has been permitted to see the treasure and to have been the means of winning it. He has sacrificed his life in the contest, and he asks that a barrow, to be called Beowulf's barrow, may be raised in his memory on the cliff. Then he takes off his collar and gives it to Wiglaf, with his helmet, ring and corselet. He will be the last survivor of the Wægmunding family when Beowulf dies.

After these words, Beowulf's soul takes its departure. It is a sad day for Wiglaf. True, the dragon was stopped for ever of his mischief: but the beloved king has paid for victory with his life.

The ten cowards emerge from the wood and gaze on Wiglaf and the dead body of the king. Wiglaf reproaches them. They have proved themselves unworthy of the armour they wear and the presents they have received from their lord. Beowulf had managed to quell the dragon single-handed, with such slight but willing help as Wiglaf could give him. He foreshadows their miserable fate.

2602 Wiglaf (also 2631, 2745, 2852, 2862), son of Weohstan and last of the Wægmundings (2607), a Swedish tribe to which Beowulf belonged. Weohstan (also 2613, 2752, 2862) fought for Onela against the Geats and slew Ohthere's son Eanmund, whose armour he was granted by Onela as part of the latter's spoils of war.

2603 Scylfings, the Swedish royal family.

2604 Ælfhere, kinsman of Wiglaf, assumed to be the true Beowulf of the poem.

2611 Eanmund, Swedish prince, son of Ohthere and brother of Eadgils. It is Eanmund's sword that Wiglaf is now wielding.

2612 Ohthere (also 2928, 2932), elder son of Ongentheow, succeeded his father as king of the Scylfings, but after his death his brother Onela seized the throne, driving out Ohthere's sons Eanmund and Eadgils. They were given refuge at the Geatish court by Heardred, whom Onela attacked for this act of hospitality. In the fight Eanmund and Heardred were killed, and Onela left the kingdom in Beowulf's charge. Eadgils, the surviving son of Ohthere was befriended by Beowulf, who aided him in his successful attempt to gain the Swedish throne and who slew the usurper Onela.

2616 Onela (also 2932), Swedish king, son of Ongentheow and younger brother of Ohthere; took a daughter of the Danish king Healfdene to wife; slain in vengeance for his usurpation of the Swedish throne and attack on Heardred and Eanmund.

2619 This ironic remark points out that Onela did not claim *wergild* or seek vengeance from Weohstan, as in other circumstances he ought to have done inasmuch as Weohstan had killed Onela's close kinsman, his nephew Eanmund: but Onela was himself trying to kill Eanmund.

2680 *Nægling*, Beowulf's sword, which he took from Dæghrefn, the standard-bearer of the Hugas and likely slayer of Hygelac during the latter's disastrous expedition.

2805 Hronesnæs (also 3136), headland on the Geatish coast where Beowulf's funeral barrow was erected.

The Battle of Ravenswood and the Death of Ongentheow [2922–98]

Wiglaf's messenger predicts troublesome days ahead for the Geats when the Franks and Frisians hear of Beowulf's death. Neither are the Swedes to be trusted. He then refers to the Geatish invasion of Sweden (under Hæthcyn and Hygelac). Such was the origin of the feud and the enmity which the Swedes are –so the messenger says– likely to remember when they hear that Beowulf is dead.

The 'Battle of Ravenswood and Death of Ongentheow', belong to the history of the Geats and Swedes. Hrethel, like his contemporary Healfdene the Dane, has three sons and one daughter. The eldest son Herebeald is accidentally killed by Hæthcyn, who, when shooting an arrow, misses his aim and strikes his brother instead (2435 ff.). The grief caused by this tragic fate that has to go unavenged eats away at the king's life. Upon his death and the succession of Hæthcyn, war breaks out between the Geats and Swedes (2472 ff., 2922 ff.). It is started by the Swedes, who attack their southern neighbours and after inflicting severe damage return home. A punitive expedition into the land of the Swedes led by Hæthcyn and Hygelac, though initially successful (even Ongentheow's queen is taken prisoner), seems destined to utter failure; the 'aged and awesome' (2929) king of the Swedes falls upon Hæthcyn's army, rescues his queen, kills the Geat king and forces his troops to seek refuge in the woods (*Hrefnesholt* 2935), threatening them all night long with death in the morning by the sword and the gallows. But at dawn the valorous Hygelac appears with his division and inspires such a terror that the Swedes flee to their fastness, pursued by the Geats. Ongentheow in a brave fight against two brothers, Eofor and Wulf, loses his life. Hygelac, now king of the Geats, on his homecoming richly repays the brothers and gives his only daughter as wife to Eofor.

The victory at Ravenswood in the year 510 ensured the Geats peace with the Swedes, who seem to have dreaded the power of the warlike Hygelac.

2924 Ongentheow (also 2951, 2961, 2986), Swedish king, father of Ohthere and Onela; slain by Eofor, a Geat.

2925 Hæthcyn, second son of Hrethel; he accidentally shot his brother, Herebald. Hrethel, king of the Geats; father of Hygelac; Beowulf's maternal grandfather. *Hrefnawudu* or *Hrefnesholt* (2935), Ravenswood, where the Swedes were decisively defeated by the Geats under Hygelac in 510 and made peace with them. The Geats (also 2991), a tribe in southern Sweden, Beowulf's people.

2927 Scylfing, Swedish royal family; in the plural, the Swedes.

2943 Hygelac (also 2952, 2958, 2977, 2988), maternal uncle of Beowulf.

2964 Eofor (also 2993, 2997), Geatish warrior, son of Wonred and brother of Wulf; slayer of the Swedish king Ongentheow, and rewarded with marriage to Hygelac's daughter. Wulf (also 2993), son of Wonred; fought Ongentheow. Wonred (also 2971), a Geat, father of Eofor and Wulf.

2965 Wulf (also 2993), son of Wonred; fought Ongentheow. Wonred (also 2971), a Geat, father of Eofor and Wulf.

The Funeral Pyre [3110–82]

Wiglaf obtains wood from the neighbouring notables, with which to kindle the funeral pyre of the great warrior-chief who had taken part in so many battles.

Seven thanes are chosen to carry away the treasures from the cave. They push the dragon over the cliff and load a wagon with the valuables. The body of Beowulf is also borne away to the promontory on which the funeral pyre is to be lit.

The Geats make a funeral pyre, placing the body of their lord in the midst of a heap of armour, and set fire to it. The roaring of the flames mingles with the weeping of the people.

Then they construct a barrow, covering the remains, and in it they place the riches they had taken from the hoard.

Twelve chieftains ride round the barrow, lamenting their king in a dirge and praising him for his manliness, his mildness and his longing to be worthy of men's praise.

The Fight at Finnsburh

The Fight at Finnsburh shares the same narrative elements as the *Tale of Finn* in *Beowulf* (1068–1159) though the *Tale* in *Beowulf* begins at a point after the events in *Finnsburh* have taken place. Yet, despite the allusive nature of the account in *Beowulf*, it is clear that Hnæf and Finn were on opposing sides (1080–5) and the fight took place at night (1076–7).

In the *Beowulf* account there is no indication that Hnæf and his warriors were defending themselves within a hall against an attack from outside; but it agrees with this assumption, if the reference to Finn's inability to 'dislodge' the Danish survivors (1082–5) is taken to mean that Hengest and his men had in fact been doing so.

The events of the first battle are partially recounted in *The Fight at Finnsburh*, which tells of an attack upon warriors led by Hnæf (40) and who include Hengest

(17). The attack takes place by night with the moon shining (7), and the warriors are defending themselves within a hall (28), whose doors they guard (14–23). The identity of the assailants is not revealed, but the conflict takes place at Finn's stronghold (36). This is evidently the battle in which Finn is slain, for whom Hildeburh mourns in the *Tale of Finn* in *Beowulf* (1076–9).

ROYAL GENEALOGIES

The Danes

- Scyld Scefing
  - Beowulf Scylding
    - Healfdene
      - Heorogar
        - Heoroweard
      - Hrothgar m. Wealhtheow Helming
        - Hrethric
        - Hrothmund
        - Freawaru m. Ingeld the Heathobard
      - Halga m. Onela Scylfing
        - Hrothulf
      - Yrse

The Geats

- Hrethel
  - Herebeald
  - Hæthcyn
  - Hygelac m. Hygd
    - daughter m. Eofor Wonreding
    - Heardred
  - daughter m. Ecgtheow Wægmunding
    - Beowulf the Geat

The Swedes

Ongentheow

Ohthere — Onela m. Yrse Scylding

Ohthere: Eanmund — Eadgils

The Heathobards

Froda — Ingeld m. Freawaru Scylding

The Half-Danes

Hoc

Hnæf — Hildeburh m. Finn the Frisian

The Frisians

Folcwalda

Finn

son

INDEX OF NAMES

Heaþolaf a Wylfing slain by Ecgtheow, Beowulf's father 460.

Heaþo-Ræmas a people living in south-eastern Norway (Romerike) 519.

Heaðo-Scilfingas Battle-Scylfings (Swedes), a by-name for the Swedish ruling house 63; 2205.

Helmingas family to which Wealtheow, Hrothgar's queen, belongs; apparently part of the Wylfings 620.

Hem(m)ing a kinsman of Eomer and Offa 1944, 1961.

Hengest leader of the Half-Danes after Hnæf's death; possibly the historical Hengest who founded the Anglo-Saxon kingdom of Kent in the mid-fifth century 1083; 1127.

Heorogar, Heregar, Hiorogar king of the Danes, son of Healfdene and elder brother of Hrothgar 61; 467; 2158.

Heorot, Heort, Hiorut hall built by Hrothgar, the Danish king; probably situated near Lejre in Zealand 78 *et passim.*

Heoroweard son of Heorogar, the Danish king, but apparently too young to succeed him 2161.

Herebeald eldest son of Hrethel, the Geatish king; accidentally killed by his younger brother Hæthcyn 2434.

Heregar see *Heorogar.*

Heremod an early Danish king, whose promise of a brilliant career deteriorated into a notoriously bad one; following Heremod's death at the hands of the Jutes, Scyld Scefing was sent to restore the Danish fortunes 901; 1709.

Hereric uncle of Heardred, the Geatish king, and probably brother of queen Hygd 2206.

Here-Scyldingas War-Scyldings (Danes), descriptive by-name for the Danish ruling house 1108.

Hetware Chattuarii, a warlike people, apparently part of the Frankish hegemony on the Lower Rhine at this time 2363; 2916.

Higelac see *Hygelac.*

Hildeburh daughter of Hoc and sister of Hnæf the 'Half-Dane'; married to Finn, the Frisian king 1071; 1114.

Hiorot see *Heorot.*

Hnæf leader of the Half-Danes; son of Hoc and brother of Hildeburh; slain in the fight at Finnsburh 1069; 1114; *Fight* 2, 40.

Hoc father of Hildeburh and Hnæf 1076.

Hondscioh a Geatish warrior and member of Beowulf's *comitatus*; slain by Grendel 2076.

Hrædla see *Hreðel.*

Hrefnawudu (also *Hrefnesholt*) 'Ravenswood', a forest in Sweden; site of a battle in which the Swedish king Ongentheow slew Hæthcyn, the Geatish king 2925; 2935.

Hreosnabeorh an unidentified hill in Geatland; site of an attack by the Swedes on the Geats 2477.

Hreðel, Hrædel, Hrædla king of the Geats, father of Hygelac and maternal grandfather of Beowulf 374 *et passim.*

Hreþling son of Hrethel 1923 (Hygelac); 2925 (Hæthcyn).

Scyldingas, *Scildingas*, *Scildungas* 'sons of Scyld', the name of the Danish ruling house, and applied generally to the Danes; several compound by-forms 53 *et passim.*

Scylfing, *Scilfing* a Swede (Ongentheow) 2487; 2968.

Scylfingas, *Scilfingas* name of the Swedish ruling house, applied generally to the Swedes; several compound by-forms 63 *et passim.*

Secgan a people *Fight* 24.

Sigeferð one of Hnæf's wariors *Fight* 15.

Sigemund legendary dragon-slayer; son of Wæls, uncle (and father) of Fitela 875.

Sige-Scyldingas Victory-Scyldings (Danes), a by-name for the Danish ruling house 597; 2004.

Suð-Dene South Danes 463; 1996.

Sweon Swedes, living in the east-central part of what is now Sweden, to the north of the great lakes 2472; 2958; 3001.

Sweoðeode the Swedish people 2922.

Swerting uncle or grandfather of Hygelac, the Geatish king 1203.

Swiorice the Swedish realm; Sweden 2383; 2495.

Þeod-Scyldingas the race of Scyldings (Danes), the Danish ruling house 1019.

Unferð son of Ecglaf, and an officer (*þyle*) at Hrothgar's court; responsible for the death of his brother 499; 530; 1165; 1488.

Wægmundingas family to which Beowulf, Wiglaf and Wihstan belong; apparently related to the Geatish ruling house 2607; 2814.

Wæls father of Sigemund, the dragon-slayer 897.

Wælsing 'son of Wæls' (Sigemund) 877.

Wealhþeo(w) wife of Hrothgar, the Danish king, and mother of Hretheric and Hrothmund 612 *et passim.*

Wederas, *Weder-Geatas* Weather-Geats, a by-name for the Geats 341 *et passim.*

Wedermearc land of the Weder-Geatas 298.

Weland famous weapon-smith of Germanic legend 455.

Wendlas, *Wendle* Vandals, remnants of whom remained in the Baltic region, at Vendel in central Sweden and elsewhere 348.

Weohstan, *Weoxtan* see *Wihstan.*

West-Dene West Danes 383, 1578.

Wiglaf, *Wilaf* a Wægmunding (the last), son of Wihstan, a kinsman and heir to Beowulf; kinsman of Ælfhere 2602 *et passim.*

Wilfingas see *Wylfingas.*

Wiðergyld a Heathobard warrior 2051.

Wonred a Geat, father of Eofor and Wulf 2971.

Wonreding 'son of Wonred' (Wulf) 2965.

Wulf a Geatish warrior; son of Wonred and brother of Eofor 2965; 2993.

Wulfgar Vandal prince, and officer at Hrothgar's court 348, 360.

Wylfingas, *Wilfingas* a Germanic people living along the southern Baltic coast 461.

Yrmenlaf a Dane, younger brother of Æschere 1324.

Yrse daughter of Healfdene, Danish king, married to Onela, the Swedish king 62.

SELECT BIBLIOGRAPHY

Editions

Beowulf, with the Finnsburg Fragment, ed. A J Wyatt and R W Chambers (Cambridge, 1914; 2nd edn., 1936).

Beowulf and the Fight at Finnsburg, ed. F. Klaeber (3rd edn. Boston, 1936).

Beowulf, with the Finnesburg Fragment, ed. C L Wrenn (London, 1958).

Beowulf, ed. Michael Swanton (Manchester, 1978).

Beowulf – A Student Edition, ed. George Jack (Oxford, 1994).

Translations

Bradley, S A J: *Anglo-Saxon Poetry* (London, Melbourne, and Toronto, 1982). In prose. Contains *Beowulf*.

Donaldson, E T: *Beowulf* (London, 1967). In prose.

Gordon, R K: *Anglo-Saxon Poetry* (London, revd. edn., 1954). In prose. Contains *Beowulf*.

Hall, J C R: *Beowulf and The Fight at Finnsburg* (London, 1901). In prose.

Lehmann, R P M: *Beowulf* (Austin, Texas, 1988). In alliterative verse.

Leonard, W E: *Beowulf* (New York, 1923). In metre imitating the *Nibelungen* couplet.

Spaeth, J D: *Old English Poetry* (Princeton, 1922). In alliterative verse. Contains *Beowulf*.

Strong, A: *Beowulf* (London, 1925). In long rhymed couplets used by William Morris in *Sigurd the Volsung*.

Critical studies

Bliss, A J: *The Metre of Beowulf* (Oxford, 1958).

Bonjour, A: *The Digressions in Beowulf*. Medium Ævum Monographs (Oxford, 1950).

Brodeur, A G: *The Art of Beowulf* (Berkeley, California, 1959).

Garmonsway, G N, J Simpson and H E Davidson, *Beowulf and its Analogues* (London, 1968).

Girvan, R: *Beowulf and the Seventh Century* (London, 1935).

Green, C: *Sutton Hoo: the Excavation of a Royal Ship-burial* (London and New York, 1963).

Kiernan, K S: *The Thorkelin Transcripts of Beowulf*. Anglistica 25 (Copenhagen, 1986).

Lawrence, W W: *Beowulf and the Epic Tradition* (Cambridge, Mass., 1928).

Malone, K: *The Thorkelin Transcripts of Beowulf*. Early English Manuscripts in Facsimile 1 (Copenhagen, 1951).

Whitelock, D: *The Audience of Beowulf* (Oxford, 1951).